Praise for *The Ho* ~~~~~~~~~~~~~~~~~~ *Business,* Educational and Military Leaders

"An inspirational self improvement guide well blended with aeronautical concepts, from an author who truly understands both arenas."

James E. Arndt, CW5 (Ret)
U.S. Army Master Aviator,
Special Operations Blackhawk Pilot in Command

"If you're interested in personal peak performance, Ken Gryske has lived it and has now translated for us all the science of *leaning forward* in life!"

James D. Murphy – CEO of Afterburner Inc.,
author of *Flawless Execution*
Former Air Force F-15 Fighter Pilot

"*The Hover Trap* by Ken Gryske is a practical tool that can help you identify your personal mission and challenge you to live a life of purpose and intention. The end game is a better life reinvented just for you. I highly recommend this book."

John Bradley Jackson, Entrepreneur, Professor, Author
Center for Entrepreneurship, Cal State University, Fullerton

"*The Hover Trap* confronts, what I think is the worst word in the English dictionary: Complacency. Effectively drawing on the corollary of hovering and taking action, the author superbly takes the reader from reactively busy to purposefully successful."

Tom Grune, VP of Sales: Americas
Microchip Technology, Inc.

"The author tells a story of triumph over difficult circumstances, highlighting the unlimited possibilities for those who demonstrate discipline and perseverance. You will want to share this story with your friends and family."

Barry Rahimian, President
SY Technology

"Adventure, danger and intense focus. Gryske brings these attributes about his flying career directly in line with our human nature and how to get the most out of ourselves. I recommend it for any professional wanting to operate at their optimum.

John Hall, President
Advanced Career Strategies

"Ken has written a thoroughly engaging book using his Blackhawk Helicopter metaphor and the science of "hovers" to deliver knowledge, wisdom and techniques about how to become the pilot of your life."

Jordan Goldrich, Partner
CUSTOMatrix, Inc.

"This is a 'Keep on your desk' book and is mandatory reading for my executive team. In these challenging economic times, we can all use a deep inward look at our lives and our careers for getting the most out of both."

Rob Healy, Co-Founder and Managing Partner
Chicago Growth Partners, West Point '86,
Harvard Business School '94

"While giving you an exciting inside view of his experiences as an Army Aviator, Ken Gryske and *The Hover Trap* challenges you to recognize the traps in our lives that hold us back from achieving our most important goals."

Brian Kenney, Boeing 777 Captain/Check Pilot
Former USMC Fighter Pilot

The Hover Trap

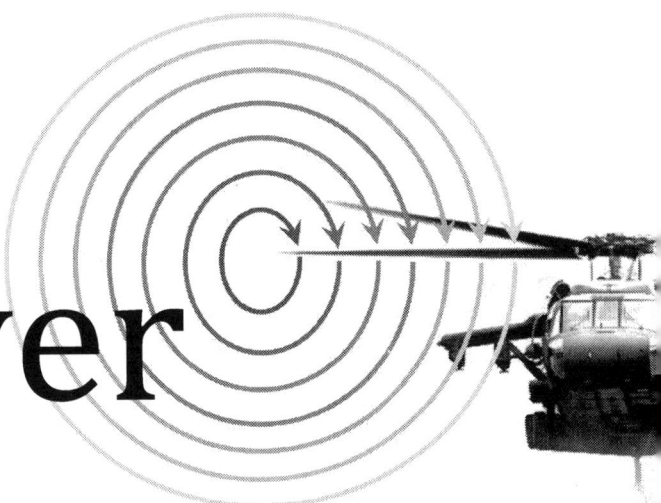

Transforming
Busy into Effective

Ken Gryske

Dru Blair©

*Tom —
Best of luck
with
Xplore!*

Kenneth R. Gryske

The Hover Trap

Published by Solutions Press
4533 MacArthur Blvd., #200
Newport Beach, CA 92660

Second edition printed June 2013

ISBN: 978-1-4664125-8-3

Printed in the United States of America
By Create Space

This is a work of non-fiction. The ideas presented are those of the author alone. All references to possible results to be gained from the techniques discussed in this book relate to specific past examples and are not necessarily representative of any future results specific individuals may achieve.

TABLE OF CONTENTS

DEDICATIONS

To my wife, for her steadfast love and support, without which I would be greatly diminished.

To my mother, who taught me to strive for the difficult, but important things in life.

To my son, who inspires me and keeps me young. Nothing is out of your reach.

ACKNOWLEDGEMENTS

I firmly believe success is a team sport and this book is no different. First I must thank Polly and Chandler Gryske, my wife and son, for showing me support and patience during this project. A special thank you goes to my mother Sonia, who has always challenged me to be my best.

Writing this book allowed me for the first time to really go back and remember my time in the service. With the perspective of almost two decades, I can say emphatically, I served with truly exceptional people: James Arndt, Kevin Lemke, Rob Healy, John Vogel, CSM Greg Chambers, Rick Vallieres, Mike Richardson, Mark Adolph, Tim Sisil, Tom Beheler, Marcus Alberghini, Curt Wallace, Mark Kranz, Paul Stuart, Colonels Tackaberry, Riding, Ottie, and "Bend-um" Borum. I especially want to thank Brad Snowden LTC(Ret) for the many conversations and expert opinions during this process. There's just too many to mention them all here. Lastly, a special thank you to Buck "Buckshot" Frazier, my primary instructor pilot who survived teaching me how to fly.

There was a huge cast of folks who read and reread draft after draft that made the book better. Thank you to Taylor Waters, Debbie Millsap and Bailey Crumpler. To Matt and Amy Wickstrom special thanks for the office space away from the distractions of life. Also, thank you to Sabrina Osborne of ArtBark Creative for designing such an engaging book cover. Also I want to thank Peter Eggertsen and Mike Brenhaug for their constant encouragement.

I must especially thank Lee Pound for coaching me through this incredible process, for editing this book and helping with the design. He was with me every step of the way and this book would not have happened without his patient guidance and thoughtful mentorship.

Lastly, I want to acknowledge those who have served, will serve, and are serving now in the Aviation Branch of the U.S. Army. Every day and night, in training or in combat, these brave individuals hurtle themselves through space, risking everything for their country and you. Rest assured and be thankful these individuals are NOT in a Hover Trap!

PREFACE

If you are stuck in your life, relationship, or work, *The Hover Trap* is for you. If you're busier than ever, can't move forward, or seem to be in a perpetual stall, keep reading.

In this book you will learn proven techniques that will get you unstuck. These techniques incorporate my two great passions; the unique characteristics of military helicopters and helping others achieve happiness and success in life. I wanted to help create a step-by-step guidebook for you. With these steps, you can manage all of the critical aspects of your life and career by becoming the Pilot in Command of YOU!

Photo 1 Full of youthful hubris, 1ˢᵗ Lieutenant Gryske at Fort Hunter-Liggett, located NW of Paso Robles, CA. (Via Author)

To accomplish this, you must be more than merely busy, you must be effective. Why? We are living through a historic era of accelerated social, technological, and economic change. To survive these changes, you must stop taking self-defeating actions, infuse yourself with the bold and audacious spirit of Army Aviation, and use the tools I present here to transform your actions from busy to effective, which will immeasurably improve your life.

As a military aviator, I discovered the many ways the unique capabilities and limitations of the modern helicopter apply to our business and personal lives. These peculiar machines are designed to perform tasks conventional airplanes can't. One of the most unique is the ability to hover. It looks easy, just as our personal hover looks easy. However, hovering is one of the most inefficient flight profiles a helicopter or a person can perform because it takes an enormous amount of energy. In this book, I'll reveal the secrets of the hover traps we all experience and show you how to use these secrets to unlock three critical keys to success in life:

- Knowing when you're stuck in, and the extraordinary cost of, a hover trap
- Knowing what kind of hover trap you are in
- Most important, knowing how to get out of a hover trap and get on with your life

As a Business Development Coach and Consultant, my goal is not to make you an aeronautical engineer. Instead, I will use the real-life metaphor of the helicopter to show you how to get from where you are to where you want to be. You will learn how hovering in your life or career takes significantly more energy than moving forward, even at a moderate pace, and why that happens.

These hover concepts will give you tools to assess your current situation, develop a plan, and use a repeatable process to accomplish your personal or career goals, large or small, every time. Make the practical techniques outlined in this book part of your personal and professional tool kit and no matter what stage of life you are in, these hover concepts will take you from stuck to productive success.

For "twenty somethings":
- See your life in a strategic context
- Learn and take advantage of key life and career management dynamics
- Create a sustainable competitive advantage in your life and career

For mid-lifers: With technology and globalization, you must always be at the top of your game. It's at this stage that a hover trap can scuttle everything you have worked for.
- Keep your eye on the ball
- Build momentum
- Guard against complacency

For senior leaders (I see special value): For you it's about your legacy and finishing well.
- Understanding the hover concepts will keep you at your optimum
- Help you make the best decisions for you and your organization
- Allow you to detect and monitor hovering behavior in your subordinates, friends, and family.

For all:
You will rediscover lessons you learned long ago but forgot. These hover concepts will deepen your perspective and shed light on habits you may not know you have.

You will create a firm, fully vetted reason for what you are meant to accomplish in your life. You will sidestep the many self-inflicted obstacles that block you from the fulfilled life you want. Is there a way to have it all? 100%! Absolutely!

Not long ago, Pastor Chris Pritchett, a talented speaker and teacher, emphasized the difference between an adventure and a quest. An adventure is fun and exciting. We might risk a little and learn a new insight or two but an adventure always brings us back to where we started. A vacation is a typical adventure. We go away, relax, meet nice people, see nice places and return refreshed for a short time.

A quest, on the other hand, transforms us. A quest compels us forward even when the outcome is in doubt. We face severe challenges, meet our worst fears, and risk much during this journey. Like heat to iron, a quest changes us forever. We are at once the same and different. We are stronger. We see our lives from a different perspective.

This book facilitates this change in perspective. At the end of each chapter, watch for this Hover Check icon:

Hover   *Check*

Below it is a short exercise that guides you to apply the hover concepts to your situation, optimize your performance, maximize all aspects of your life, and help you transform your busyness into effectiveness.

Life is not too short. It is too long to be stuck in a hover. It should not be a tedious slog through time. It should be an audacious and vibrant quest.

Enjoy this book the same way I loved flying: low, fast, and above all else, to accomplish the mission.

FOREWORD

The hardest part of learning to fly a helicopter for me was the hover...the perfect equilibrium of lift and gravity, of thrust and drag...and it takes a lot of practice to perfect the maneuver.

This book will show you how to take the concept of hovering a helicopter and apply it to your life so that you will NOT HAVE TO STAY IN A HOVER! This book will show you a blueprint for taking control of your life and moving it in the direction YOU want to take it.

The author has done a superb job of providing a workbook-like, step by step process for all of us to follow. It is especially useful for those of us that have not decided what we want in our lives, where to do it, or how to get there.

After reading this book, I was taken aback by how useful the correlation between flying a UH-60 Blackhawk helicopter and piloting my life can be.

Read the book with an eye on where you are in your life. Are you in a hover, not moving forward or backward? Are you flying forward, knowing where you will land next?

This book will help you get to where you want to go.

James H. Pillsbury
Lieutenant General (Ret)
Former Deputy Commanding General,
U.S. Army Materiel Command,
Army Aviator

CHAPTER 1

Danger in the Hover

I stared with panicked detachment through the helicopter windshield. Straight ahead the ground filled my view. I hung there as though at the highest point of a pendulum's swing. Suspended, tail up, nose down, I knew my aircraft was seconds from crashing.

As I anticipated the downward slide, time slowed and I became aware of strange details. A tuft of grass, blown flat by the rotor wash, danced in slow motion. A mist of red Alabama dust skittered over the ground. This could not be good.

My hearing was muffled, my vision narrowed, my arms and legs moved with the grace of a rusted gate as sweat ran down my neck and back. My aviator RayBans hid my eyes, now wider than silver dollars. The army aviator thing was quickly becoming the worst idea I had ever had.

"I have the controls, Lieutenant Gryske."

Who is that? I thought.

"I HAVE THEM!" the instructor insisted.

I let go of the controls and regained my ability to breathe. The instructor took control of the helicopter, a Vietnam vintage UH-1 Huey as old as me, and settled it down to a calm and sane standard three-foot hover. He was talking to me. I looked at him. In a matter-of-fact, calm, and almost bored manner, he explained how hovering would soon become second nature to me. I felt only relief at still being alive. For the first time in my young life, I felt delivered from certain death, until he said, "Not bad. Keep your scan going. Pick two reference points. You have the controls."

"Are you kidding me?!"

In a matter of seconds I was out of control in all three axes. In aviation speak I had departed controlled flight. Again.

This inglorious first training session took place in 1989 just outside the fence of Lowe Army Airfield at Fort Rucker, Alabama. Following it were years of incredible challenge and success. But on that day, like many of my classmates, I was at the beginning of a steep and steady learning curve.

Hovering is the most difficult task a helicopter pilot can master. It balances all of the forces acting on the helicopter. Lift equals weight, thrust equals drag - equilibrium.

Not only is hovering extremely difficult, the act of hovering is very inefficient, in a helicopter and in life.

We spend enormous amounts of energy trying to maintain balance in our lives, trying to maintain the hover. It's time to get out of the hover and the hover traps which keep us there.

The Mistake We're All Programmed to Make

Our culture celebrates equilibrium and balance. Let me ask you a few questions:

- Should you strive to be a well-rounded person?
- Is it preferable to have a well-balanced meal?
- Does our government have a system of checks and balances?

Balancing our tires, diets, checkbooks, and lives is a good thing. In fact, thousands of self-help books exist espousing the virtues of balance, or equilibrium.

A *Journal of Personality and Social Psychology* article entitled, "Navigating Personal and Relational Concerns: The Quest for Equilibrium" (Kumashiro, Rusbult, & Finkel, 2008), says people move themselves toward equilibrium in personal and relationship wants and needs, increasing their psychological, physical, and relational well-being. It's good for us to be in balance, in equilibrium, or in a hover, right? Of course it is, most of the time.

The problem arises when we are so comfortable in our hover that we fight to stay there even when we've triggered a growth mode. That's the hover trap I'm alluding to: Simply staying too long in our comfort zones.

We dig in instead of moving out smartly. Why? Some of us don't even know we are doing it. Others have difficulty with change. Still others are just plain afraid.

Ground School

Family, friends, careers, health, and one's spiritual life encapsulate every aspect of who we are. It's vital that we live our lives in a fulfilling way that enhances our wellbeing and success in all its forms. Only then can we derive satisfaction from it.

We are complicated beings. What goes on between our ears makes a sophisticated helicopter look incredibly simple. Our lives, and how we act and react, are complex, situational, and uniquely individual. In Figure 1-1, I outline the most important aspects of life. You may have others. Please add them. This book is for you.

I approach life and the hover traps that follow from this perspective. We will not discuss these aspects individually.

However, by reading this book, you will uncover universal truths that, if applied vigorously, will have a profound and lasting positive effect on your happiness, accomplishments, and, ultimately, your success.

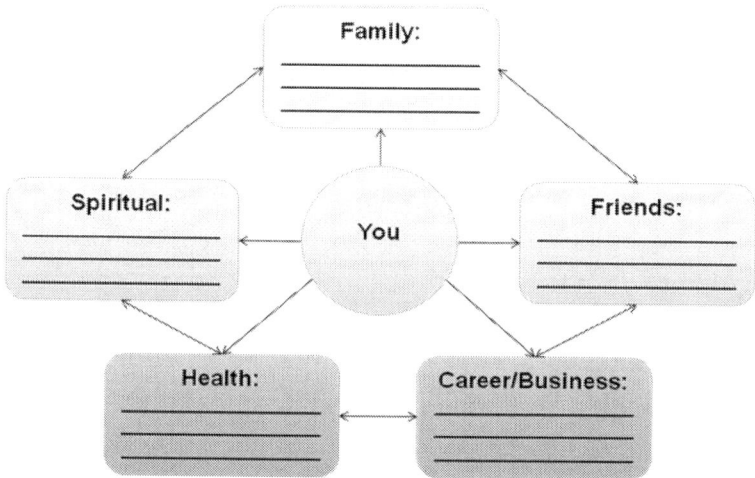

Figure 1-1: For illustration purposes, the critical life aspects are broken out separately. In practice, as the arrows indicate, they are all interconnected. Distress in one aspect often affects one or all the others.

The helicopter metaphor allows us to examine this subject objectively while enabling us to apply these lessons to more personal and emotionally charged areas of our lives. What can be more fraught with emotion, rationalization, blame, shame, and fear than feeling stuck in our lives without a clear path forward?

Inspiration comes from many places. During coaching sessions with my clients and from my own experiences in the military, business, and as an Executive Coach, I recognized that many of my clients' situations were similar to hovering. This observation jogged a faint memory long ago set aside. I climbed into my attic, found my old UH-60 Operators Manual, untouched for more than a decade, and searched the performance charts. I found what I was looking for and I was right:

- It takes the same amount of power to hover a UH-60 Blackhawk as it does to fly it at 138 mph.
- Additionally, flying at 74 mph requires 30% less power than hovering.
- Why?

Figure 1-2: Sikorsky UH-60A Blackhawk

Those two facts and the question, "Why?" vividly illustrate dynamics you experience every day but do not even recognize. I assure you, a hover is not what you think. Together, we're going to uncover hover traps by asking and answering the following questions:

- What are we all programmed to do?
- What's the mistake we all make and why?
- What are hover traps and how do we avoid them?
- Am I in a hover trap right now?
- How do I get out of one and stay out of it?
- What obstacles will I face?

This is a workbook. You will complete exercises throughout it to drive home the issues that are most important to you. Don't simply read this book, utilize it.

Boiled down to its core, this book is about change, not just any change, but the kind of change that has profound, long-term positive effects on your life. That kind of change requires hard work. Not everyone will do what's required. If you do, you will have a competitive advantage for the rest of your life. You will see that hover traps keep you so busy you're too preoccupied or exhausted to be effective.

You may wonder why I'm using the metaphor of a US Army helicopter. I admit it's not the most touchy-feely image I could have come up with, but I have my reasons. Paramount among them is my experience.

I commanded a 15-aircraft, rapid deployable air assault unit nicknamed the Knight Warriors. I've flown the Blackhawk in some of the most demanding mission conditions from night vision goggle, Nap of the Earth counter-narcotic missions on our southern border to naval deck-landings in the Pacific Ocean.

Mission is everything. It gives us purpose, direction, and serves to direct our limited resources to the achievement of our goals.

Photo 1-1 Counter narcotics mission on the US-Mexican border. Author is fourth from right. The skull hangs in the author's garage. (Via Author)

Military flying, including Army Aviation, does not exist for its own sake. There is always a mission to accomplish. Mission accomplishment is the only reason this book exists. Your personal mission, whatever it is, has driven you to pick it up. You're searching. Together we will find answers.

Air Assault operations are bold and audacious. There is an esprit-de-corps I was lucky enough to experience and want to share with you. This dauntless spirit is the secret sauce to success, easy to talk about yet hard to find. Organizations and individuals that possess it have a competitive advantage that can't be easily manufactured.

The image of a Blackhawk flying a tactical mission while avoiding detection is a compelling parallel to our life's journey.

The Blackhawk is an outstanding helicopter that's used by the Army, Air Force, Navy, Coast Guard, Customs, and some Fire Authorities. It's also used by a number of other countries including Israel, Japan, and Australia. Notably, it's the favored mount of Task Force 1-160th Special Operations Air Regiment (SOAR) - the Night Stalkers.

A simple fact: Helicopters cannot fly without a pilot. The head pilot is called the Pilot in Command (PIC). It's a skill level

---

I'd like to introduce you to the Pilot in Command of your life: YOU!

---

and responsibility designation and has nothing to do with one's rank. The PIC has ultimate responsibility. He or she calls the shots, ensures all procedures are followed, sees that the aircraft is suitable for flight, checks to make sure the flight plan is filed and that communication with air traffic control is correct. I'd like to introduce you to the Pilot in Command of your life: YOU!

Now, for this to come together, I need you to do this thought exercise:

Imagine your Blackhawk as the vehicle you use to travel your life's journey. In it, you carry your relationships, your health, your career, and any problem, task, or issue you have. This helicopter is your vehicle of choice. It's powerful, fast, and maneuverable. Paramount to this, you are the Pilot in Command.

I want to be very clear on this point. This book and the concepts in it leave room for the belief in God and the power of prayer. I strongly believe, regardless of our religious views, we first must show up, take an active role and be present. This makes perfect sense and here's why.

Pilots manipulate the helicopter controls to make the helicopter go where they want it to go. The pilot controls speed, direction, altitude, and maneuvering around and over obstacles in their flight path. He determines where the helicopter will ultimately go and has the responsibility to get it there safely. If a strong wind is pushing the helicopter off course, the pilot adjusts the controls and puts it back on course.

It's the same with your life. You are responsible for maneuvering through your life, climbing, descending, banking, accelerating, or decelerating. YOU are in control of what your helicopter does. You can't control the rest of the world, but you can control how you think, prepare, and react to it.

That's why I leave room for a higher power. There are simply some things that are completely outside of our control. The vast majority of events in our lives, however, simply require us to be present and willing to take the responsibility to manage them.

I've talked to hundreds of high-performing men and women and seen, first-hand, what happens when they do not take an active role in some of the most important aspects of their lives. Have you ever seen this disengagement happen to somebody's marriage, friendships, health, or career? The results are never pretty.

Think about this: What would happen if a pilot let go of the controls of their helicopter? It might fly waywardly along for awhile, but it's guaranteed to crash and burn. Again, it's not pretty.

WTF and the Truth Room

I know firsthand what it means to settle for less and just go along. During an extended period in my career, when I was ruled by the quest for stability and *the sure thing*, I lost my way. Unbeknown to me, I allowed a disconnect to occur between my values, purpose, and what I did for a living. At the time it felt like I was aimlessly wandering in the wilderness, totally reactive, letting my helicopter fly me instead of taking the controls and flying it. If this has happened to you, you know the feeling.

I came close to crashing and burning but I didn't and you don't have to either. I had what business coach Mike Brenhaug in his book, *WTF: Transform What Appears Negative into a Positive to Become Unstoppable,* calls a "WTF Moment."(Brenhaug, 2011), It isn't what you might think.

The acronym can stand for a lot of things but Brenhaug keeps it positive. WTF means: Where's the Fun? Where's the Future? Where's the Fuel? Where's the Focus?

As Brenhaug points out, we ask ourselves these questions only after we have reached a certain discomfort threshold. I also believe we need the perspective that enables us to ask the right questions and in turn be able to answer them clearly and truthfully. I needed to tell the truth to myself about getting out of what I now know was a hover trap. To put it simply, my WTF moment was the doorway to the Truth Room.

Entrance to the Truth Room, an invention of Amy Julian, a close friend and organizational development professional, is required before any real change can happen in our lives. What is the Truth Room?

It's where you tell the truth to at least one person: YOU. It's a place in your mind where you can have an honest and frank conversation with yourself, not to beat yourself up over past failings, but to honestly assess important issues in your life. The world is full of people who are expert at constructing an inaccurate, rationalized view of themselves, their actions, and capabilities. You probably know a few of them. I urge you not to be one of them.

The reason the Truth Room is so important is because the hover traps we will talk about in this book are mostly based on actions and behaviors developed over our lifetimes. These habits steal our energy, time, and treasure and suck the enjoyment we should have from our lives.

This organizational self-awareness can be the difference between progress and survival, or decline and extinction.

Real change does not happen because somebody else wants us to change. It only happens when WE want to change. Typically, we only want to change if we think we have a real problem. The act of seeing our shortcomings can only happen when we enter the Truth Room and confront our real, *don't want to share* issues.

This concept also works well when applied to organizations. Like individuals, organizations can develop a false sense of what they are, their motives, and their capabilities. They too can be consumed with being busy and forget about being effective. At any time, leadership can use the Truth Room to face real organizational issues that are not pretty or easy to confront. This organizational self-awareness can be the difference between progress and survival or decline and extinction.

It doesn't matter if you're changing the dynamics within your family, friends, career, health or spiritual life, or changing the culture of your organization. Whether individual or organizational, change starts in the Truth Room. If you have a WTF moment, it means the door to the Truth Room is open.

Emergency Procedures

Aviators use emergency procedures to ensure survival when something fails on the aircraft. They are required to memorize the most critical procedures because there won't be time to look them up when a real emergency occurs.

The same is true in our own lives. In instances where we require immediate action, failure to act will have lasting negative consequences for us and those we care about. However, we are programmed to seek out and hover in our comfort zones, making us slow to react to changing situations.

I have included emergency procedures at the end of each chapter to show you the steps you need to take to control your situation and move forward. Remember our metaphor: You're the Pilot in Command of your helicopter and now something significant has happened to it. The longer you wait to take action the busier and more ineffective you will be. It's time for immediate action.

Hover Check

✦ What is the Truth Room?

✦ What is a Pilot in Command?

✦ Privately, list a time when you relinquished responsibility for your life.

✦ Of the following, what aspect of your life do you feel needs the most attention? Family, friends, career/business, health, spiritual life.

✦ Who's your Pilot in Command?

EMERGENCY PROCEDURE 1

IF YOU ARE <u>BUSY</u>, BUT NOT <u>EFFECTIVE</u> OR FEEL "<u>STUCK</u>" IN YOUR LIFE:

☩ Imagine your Blackhawk represents your life's journey

☩ All that is important to you is in the back. CHECK:

>   ☩ Family
>   ☩ Relationships
>   ☩ Career / Business
>   ☩ Health
>   ☩ Spiritual Life

☩ The Pilot in Command of your life is YOU!

<u>IMMEDIATELY</u> TAKE COMMAND OF YOUR AIRCRAFT

TM 55-1520-237-CL   E-1

CHAPTER 2

Feeling Trapped

Looking down at where the troops said they needed to land, all I could see was a black hole in the 100-foot pines through my night vision goggles. It looked like a tight fit as we orbited the landing zone. I'd been told the ground was pretty flat where we were preparing to descend.

After talking the plan over with the crew and emphasizing keeping the tail rotor out of the trees, I tentatively lowered the aircraft into the small clearing.

"Sir, you're going to have to move the tail to the left to fit in here," reported the crew chief. It was a very tight fit.

I told myself to relax and breathe.

"75 feet, 70 feet," the copilot read from the radar altimeter.

We were slowly descending down a vertical shaft and shifting the tail like a key in a lock. The whole time, I was thinking I had made a mistake attempting to land here, but it was too late. Staying focused was all I could do until we got closer to the ground.

"15 feet."

"Tail's clear."

"Sir, this is a slope landing."

"What?!"

I noticed a dead log being pushed uphill by our rotor wash. "*Focus.*" We were facing uphill on the side of a mountain. The left wheel touched down, then the right. The rotor disk was getting within a foot of the rising terrain to the front.

With the tail still flying, the troops jumped out and the process of slowly weaving our aircraft through the trees started. I was exhausted. My crew was tense. I was mad at myself for putting them in this situation. No escape route. No options. No margin for error.

As we cleared the trees, I transferred the controls to the other pilot and realized I had learned a lesson about flying that night. I had put myself, my crew, and the aircraft in a position where we all had to perform without error. I felt like I had dodged a bullet. That five-minute hover was the most difficult flying I have ever experienced.

Punctuated Equilibrium

With helicopters and life, hovering is inefficient and a lot of work. All this talk about hovering and hover traps — why should we care?

When hovering, a helicopter is at equilibrium. The lift the rotors produce equals the weight of the aircraft. The thrust equals the drag of the aircraft. (See Figure 2-1) It doesn't move forward or backward, up or down, or side to side. It's balanced in midair.

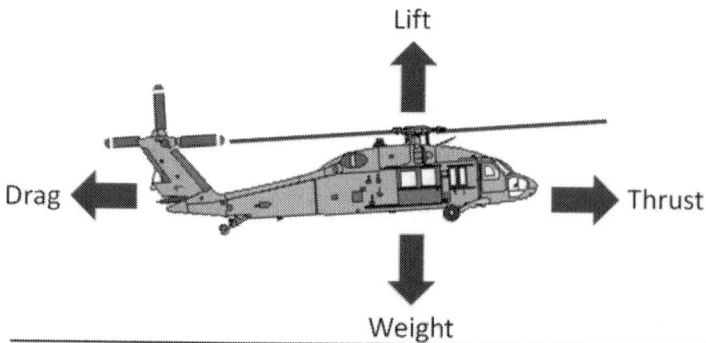

Figure 2-1 Aerodynamic forces in equilibrium during a hover

When we get into a personal hover, we do much the same thing. Our careers seem to be going nowhere. No matter what we do we are stuck in the job with no hope of getting out. Our relationships may be dull but not bad enough to get out of or bad enough to spend energy fixing. Like a hovering helicopter, we are stuck in a state of limbo and like a stationary bike, no matter how fast we pedal, we move nowhere.

This shouldn't surprise us. Our DNA, our nature as human beings, and our cultures all program us to hover.

We humans have comfort zones. When we have a choice to try something new and risky or do what we usually do, we most often choose to do the usual. A good illustration of this is the scientific concept of punctuated equilibrium.

Paleontologists Steven Jay Gould and Niles Eldredge many years ago published a seminal article, "Punctuated Equilibria: An Alternative to Phyletic *(Darwin's)* Gradualism" (S.J.Gould & Eldredge, 1972). This work, now firmly accepted in the scientific community, shows how species change, adapt, and evolve.

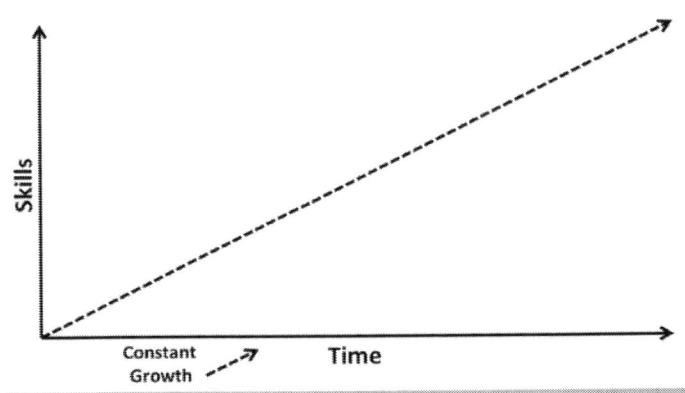

Figure 2-2 The stately unfolding, or constant progress, view of evolution

In short, two main schools of thought exist in the theory of evolution. Darwin's Gradualism states that species are always evolving in a slow, measured, and almost predestined manner, a "stately unfolding" of progress described as evolution by creeps. Figure 2-2 above illustrates this theory showing constant growth over time.

Punctuated Equilibrium states things differently. In Gould's theory, species are static most of the time. Species usually don't change. They maintain the status quo until a significant event occurs. Although Gould speaks of external events affecting the survival of a species, these events can also be initiated internally. In evolution, such an event might be the isolation of a species on an island or a huge natural disaster.

This can apply to our individual lives as well. Remember that most of the time we are content to live in our comfort zone, to keep the same job or do the same things. When an external event, such as transitioning from student to employee, preparing for a new child, or being laid off occurs we are forced to initiate change. An internally initiated event could be an individual who aspires to be promoted. She might determine that she requires new, enhanced skills to qualify for the new position, initiating her decision to enroll in some training classes.

In evolution, this event, whether internal or external, requires the species to adapt, change, and acquire new skills and capabilities to survive. Once the evolution is completed and the species is able to survive in the new environment, adaptation stops. Once again, the species enters a state of equilibrium (hover) until another event occurs. This cycle repeats again and again. Figure 2-3 shows the stepped action from being static to growth and back again.

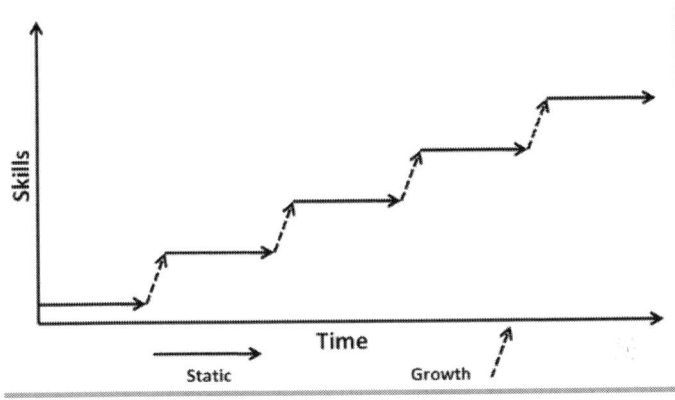

Figure 2-3 The stepped progress of Gould's Punctuated Equilibrium

The same thing can happen in our second example. Once we move into the job market, upgrade our skills and get a promotion, we settle into another hover. The idea of alternating static and growth phases resonates with me and a lot of people I work with. It also shows in a dramatic way how humans tend to hover in comfort zones and find that changing them is incredibly difficult. Gould's theory helps illustrate why we often react the way we do.

No matter what we may do, change happens. Human beings have changed and evolved in many ways over the years. For example, "Over the last 150 years, the average height of people in industrialized nations has increased approximately 10 centimeters or about four inches." (Dougherty, 1998)

Gould's theory shows that life has comfort zones, just as people have comfort zones. We tend to stay put in any given situation.

I'm interested in how we got there but I'm even more interested in how to move people out of their hover after their event happens.

Personal Development Path vs. Career Path

To avoid confusion, we must make a distinction between career and personal development paths. Although they may look very similar, they differ in significant ways.

Our personal development path includes our family, friends, career/business, health, and spiritual paths. Career paths are just one of these personal development paths and operate independently. A static or growth period in one does not necessarily correspond to a static or growth period in the other.

Once we understand that these hover traps or static periods exist in our lives, we next need to understand why we entered them, identify them, learn how to get out of them, and ultimately optimize these cycles. We can't change the fact that they happen but we can change how we react to them. This valuable life skill will give us a sustainable competitive advantage in all aspects of our lives. Figure 2-4 contrasts a hypothetical static/growth curve with an optimized one.

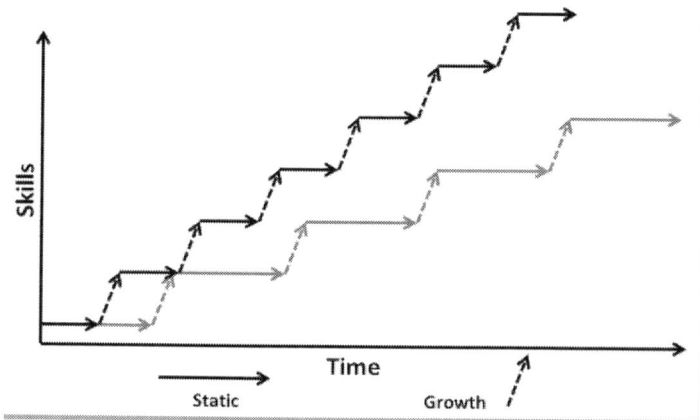

Figure 2-4 Optimized personal development chart illustrating the advantage of abbreviated static periods

I equate hovering with merely being busy. To transform it into effective behavior, we must minimize our hovers over time. We will always have times when we make no progress. However, true effectiveness arises from recognizing when these traps occur, minimizing our stay in them, and spending most of our time in a growth mode.

Steve: The Flat Liner

Recently, while I was working through the concepts outlined in this book, I spoke to a group of professionals. One man in the audience, in his late forties, caught my attention. As I spoke, I noticed that he nodded affirmatively during my discussion of Gould's Punctuated Equilibrium. I appreciated this positive, non-verbal feedback, but as I continued, he got more and more enthusiastic, to the point where I thought he might jump up and shout, "Amen, Brother!"

After the talk I approached him because I was curious to know why this particular part of my message had such a powerful impact on him. Steve told me that he had recently started to work for company and was previously VP of Sales for another company. *"Maybe it's easy to be philosophical about the last few months in my career,"* he said, *"but now I see why I was let go from my last position. I had been doing the same things over and over again, becoming complacent. I guess I ran dry on new ways of looking at what's possible. Using your words, I was stuck in 'static' mode. Getting let go was the bucket of cold water that shocked me into action. At the time, I just didn't see it, but looking back now, I can clearly see I had stalled into a hover."*

I've kept in touch with him. He is definitely in a growth phase at his new position. He's charged up and driving new initiatives throughout his organization. He's no longer the *flat liner* he once talked about. Sometimes just hearing or seeing a new message from somebody outside of your normal circle can ignite a shift in perspective and initiate a punctuated growth spurt. For Steve, hearing about Gould's theory of Punctuated Equilibrium helped him understand why he lost his previous job and what he could do to make sure that never happened again.

I hope it will do the same for you.

Hover Check

🕊 Do you feel you are in equilibrium now?

🕊 In what aspects of your life?

🕊 What external forces are acting on you?

🕊 What is the mistake we are all programmed to make?

🕊 Privately, list a time when you stayed static or hovering when you knew you should have moved on.

🕊 What was the cost of remaining static in time, energy, or opportunities?

EMERGENCY PROCEDURE 2

IF A SIGNIFICANT "EVENT" <u>EXISTS</u> OR <u>OCCURS</u> IN ANY OF THE FOLLOWING AREAS:

- Your Family

- Your Relationships

- Your Career / Business

- Your Health

- Your Spiritual Life

<u>IMMEDIATELY</u> UNDERSTAND YOU MUST LEAVE EQUILIBRIUM, YOUR COMFORT ZONE, BALANCE, OR HOVER.

CHAPTER 3

Find 30 Percent More Power

A one-dimensional monochromatic green world rushed under our aircraft, flattened because night vision goggles take away depth perception. They also intensify existing light 2,500 times, allowing pilots to fly at night. Tonight I could see everything, even the moon shadow of our aircraft as it rushed toward our objective.

The moon was hidden by a thin layer of cirrus clouds. Through the goggles, the moon illuminated the clouds, transforming them into a giant florescent light in the sky.

We flew through rugged mountain country with peaks topping 10,000 feet and few places to land in case of an emergency.

The tops of tall evergreens zipped past on either side as we flew up a valley, always climbing. To the right, a series of smaller valleys drew up to a sharp ridgeline pressing above us. Looking through the Plexiglas above me, I could see the peaks. Our objective was up there.

Bathed in low, greenish light, the cockpit was all business and no small talk.

"Sir, two clicks to the release point."

"Rappel master gives us thumbs up."

"Slide doors open."

"Turn right into the next draw."

"Clear right."

"You're clear right, sir."

"Stop turn."

"Roger. Stop turn."

We continued to climb.

Moderate turbulence buffeted us as if we were driving down an old dirt road. In the back, an 11-man squad of Long Range Surveillance Detachment (LRSD) soldiers, who had been in isolation for four days planning, rehearsing, and coming up with solutions for every imaginable contingency, waited. Their faces blacked out, they carried weapons, ammunition, food, and water to stay in these mountains for five days without resupply.

After flying for 50 minutes up the winding canyons, we would have only enough fuel to wait for 15 minutes in case the ingress team needed immediate extraction. This team was under orders to conduct surveillance on the objective and report their findings to headquarters.

Suddenly, what seemed like a giant hand grabbed our aircraft, stopping it from climbing. I applied more power and heard the engines respond, but we didn't climb. The trees were getting closer.

I added 10% more power, and then 10% more. The wind had rushed up and over the ridge in front of us and poured down on us like a waterfall. The steep mountainside filled my windscreen, scrolling down as we tried to claw our way upward.

I slowed the aircraft to Maximum Climb/Endurance airspeed. It carries two names because it is the most efficient and aerodynamic speed. In the Blackhawk, at most weights, temperatures, and altitudes, Max Climb/Endurance airspeed was around 64 knots indicated airspeed (KIAS) or about 74 mph. I set the airspeed there.

If a pilot needed to be airborne for the most time possible, he would fly at this airspeed to conserve fuel. At sea level, the combination of full power and Max Climb airspeed would produce the fastest rate of ascent, often well over 6,000 feet per minute.

"We're barely climbing!"

The engines were now in the yellow caution range as I pulled in the last of the power. The helicopter pulsated under the strain.

"I'm counting to ten. If we're not there by then, I'll right pedal turn and dive down the mountain," I announced.

Photo 3-1 Soldiers rappelling from a Blackhawk in training. It is a requirement for the Rappel Master to possess an axe or riggers knife to cut the ropes if required to save the aircraft, regardless of what or who was on the end of the rope. (Courtesy US Army)

We crested the ridgeline at seven. As we cleared the down draft, I significantly reduced power. We were now suspended on a torrent of air rushing up the front side of the mountain. We settled into a 50-foot hover.

"Ropes out."

"Men on rappel."

The helicopter rocked as the men jumped out.

"They're all clear."

"Drop ropes."

"You're clear, sir."

As I added power and pulled the nose up, the wind pushed us backward the way we came. With right pedal, the Blackhawk reared up and rotated until we were diving down the side of the mountain, picking up speed and breathing easier.

FACT 1:

*The **same** amount of power is required to **hover** a UH-60A Blackhawk at 10 feet as it takes to propel it **120 knots (138 mph)**.*

FACT 2:

*At **64 knots (74 mph)** the same helicopter requires **30% less power** than at a hover.*

Figure 3-1 UH-60A Operators Manual, Dept of Army, HQ, 1996 updated 2002

When a helicopter is hovering, it's working very hard being busy, but it's not going anywhere. To a casual observer, the aircraft will look normal, but the pilot knows how much power is needed to keep his craft suspended.

As you can see from this story, it is important to understand what is really going on when you're:

- In a hover
- Transitioning to forward flight
- In forward flight

As you read these descriptions, you will immediately recognize the strong parallels between helicopter flight and our lives (and impress your friends with your in-depth knowledge of helicopter aerodynamics).

Hovering Flight

Airplanes are simple: Go fast enough and they will fly. I like to think helicopters are a little more sophisticated. To fly, the helicopter has to lift its own weight. That takes power.

Photo 3-2 In Dru Blair's dramatic painting, the River Hawks, two Blackhawks decelerate just above the water showing the vortices created to advantage. (Photorealistic Painting Courtesy Dru Blair)

Rotors suck air from above and push it out the bottom. The action of the airflow lifts the aircraft. The air doesn't go away after it's pushed through the rotor disk; it circulates out and up to the top and gets sucked in again. This is called a vortex.

So, not only is the helicopter lifting its own weight, it is in fact also swimming upstream. That takes additional power and explains why hovering is an inefficient mode of flight. It's brute force.

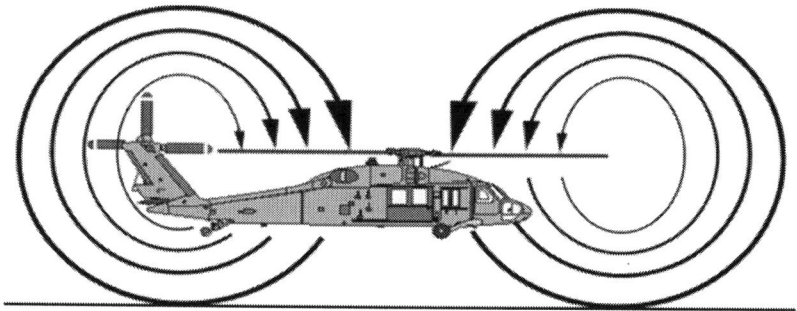

Figure 3-2 Helicopter in hovering flight

Have you ever felt like you are using brute force to just stay where you are? Hovering, or not moving forward, to resolve issues central to our well-being drains us of the only two finite resources we can manage other than money: time and energy.

When in a hover, we often confuse activity, being **busy**, using our time and energy, with being **effective, which** means we are accomplishing necessary tasks required to move closer to achieving our goals.

That is what is so tricky about the hover traps we fall into. We feel busy, harried, hurried and tired. WE DON'T FEEL LIKE WE'RE IN A HOVER. Like a hovering helicopter, we're making a lot of noise, blowing dust, consuming fuel, expending a large amount of energy, and not going anywhere. We're not moving.

Goals are fundamental to a strategy of action, moving forward with purpose, and accomplishment. During my military flying career, I never left the ground without knowing where I was going and why. Because they are so important, we will discuss goals and goal setting in more detail in a future chapter.

> *I never left the ground without knowing where I was going and why.*

When you understand the facts about hover dynamics from earlier in this chapter, you will agree that being in a hover is not the best mode from which to operate. A hover is not a resting place. It is important to recognize a hover when it happens before it takes a toll on your time, energy, and whatever issue needs your attention.

Transitioning to Forward Flight

You've decided to get out of the hover. You move your helicopter forward, but things don't go as planned. You may have moved incrementally closer to your goal, but you have put yourself back into a hover.

As humans, we feel a constant pull toward a hovering state, much like gravity tugging at our bodies. It's always there. To move forward we have to actively resist it. Have you felt that sensation before? You try to move a portion of your life forward, but an unseen resistance pulls you back to your starting point. Helicopters have the same problem.

Photo 3-3 A Blackhawk aggressively leaves the Landing Zone after delivering its troops. (Courtesy US Army)

This phenomenon, Effective Translational Lift (ETL), happens to all helicopters at very low speed while transitioning from hovering to forward flight.

Remember the vortices created while we were in the hover? (Figure 3-2) Now we're starting to move forward, but at about 18 to 27 mph, the front part of the rotor disk begins to move past the vortices and into undisturbed, smooth, or clean air.

At the same time, the rear section of the rotor disk is still in the disturbed, dirty air created by the front part of the rotor disk. *(FM 1-203 Fundamentals of Flight, Dept of Army, HQ, 1983)* The illustration in Figure 3-3 captures this concept.

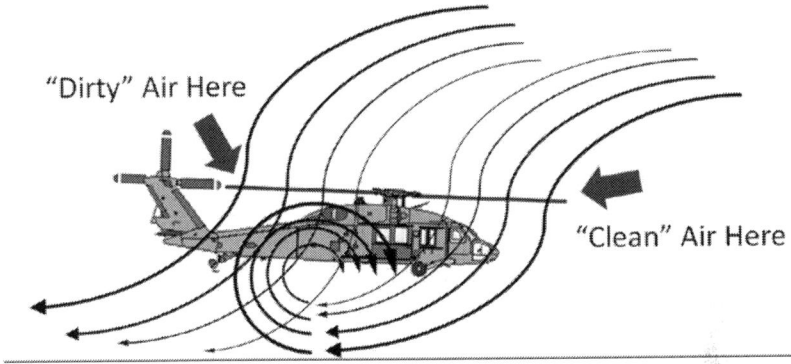

Figure 3-3 Helicopter in ETL

To move out of ETL, the pilot must anticipate and correct two aerodynamic effects:

- The nose of the aircraft will pitch upward, decelerating the aircraft.
- The aircraft will roll to the right, pointing in a different direction.

Have you ever started toward a goal or initiated a project that almost immediately stalled? When the dust settled, were you pointed in a different direction, a direction you had no intention of heading? The worst part is that you are still in an inefficient hover and still working very hard to go nowhere.

Claudia's "Ground Hog Day"

Claudia, a graphic designer at a successful communications company, experienced this exact scenario. Because of her creative ability to understand and communicate what the customer wanted, her company had recently promoted her. Now with the added responsibility to manage others and their creative processes, she quickly realized she needed a new way to look at work and enhance her skills.

"At first," she said, "I was so excited, but that quickly turned to sheer terror when the first project I was in charge of missed a critical deadline. No matter how many different approaches I tried to get that project moving forward, it kept stalling. I never worked so hard for such a small result.

"Some of my team's work styles were so different from mine I didn't even consider changing the way I interacted with them. For the first time, I was working with other departments in the company and needed their buy-in to make my projects successful.

"I thought I would make it happen. But nothing happened. It was not only scary and frustrating, it was plain exhausting."

Claudia was trapped in an inefficient hover and unsuccessfully trying to escape it. I know the feeling, and I'm sure you have experienced it too.

A lot of people go through life not understanding the dynamics of getting things done. They take off not knowing where they are going and why. They do not anticipate the ETL that they hit, so they decelerate and recover in another hover pointed in a different direction.

> *A lot of people go through life not understanding the real dynamics of getting things done.*

Instead of fixing their sights on a goal, understanding there will be obstacles, challenges, and naysayers, they promptly head off in the new direction just as unprepared as before. What happens? The same thing! They are stuck in a hover trap.

Forward Flight after ETL

To correct for ETL and a perpetual hover, the pilot must anticipate the aerodynamics of ETL and push the stick forward to stop the nose from rising. The pilot must move the stick to the left to counteract the rolling tendency to the right.

Once through ETL, the rotor system is completely in clean air, with no airflow recirculation, as in the last two flight modes.

Figure 3-4 depicts the airflow of a Blackhawk in forward flight. The airflow is more horizontal and becomes even more so as airspeed increases.

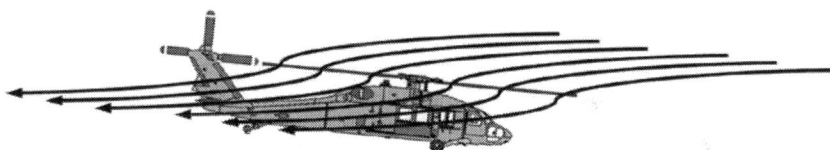

Entire Rotor Is In "Clean" Air

Figure 3-4 Helicopter in forward flight. The airflow is smooth throughout the entire rotor system, providing up to a 30% increase in efficiency

So, what's the big deal? A lot! Once the helicopter is on the other side of ETL, it gets up to a 30% increase in the rotor system's efficiency. From the data I used, and as we learned in the story that opened this chapter, the most efficient airspeed, also called, Maximum Climb/Endurance Airspeed, is 64 knots or 74 mph.

This airspeed is the most aerodynamic and uses the least amount of power and fuel, thus allowing the aircraft to stay airborne longer. Because it is the most aerodynamic speed, it will also deliver the highest rate of climb for the aircraft. Stop and ask yourself this:

✦ What is my optimum speed?

Just as we all have a unique fingerprint, we all have our own optimum speed. You need to find yours. We all need to jealously guard a reserve for when life throws a significant obstacle in front of us.

By analyzing the factors that kept returning her to a hover trap and determining what adjustments she needed to make, Claudia found her optimum speed and became a better planner and anticipator of obstacles inherent to her new position. Her department now runs projects on time with increased customer satisfaction. She learned the art of breaking through ETL to capture the efficiencies on the other side.

Applying this concept to our own situations can show us the pace we need to control our lives. What actions may we need to do differently? What might we need to cut out? Applied to career advancement, time for relationship maintenance, or working out, continuing to indefinitely fly at our fastest possible speed will only lead to exhaustion, burnout and, ultimately, a crash.

Granted, the speed may not be blistering, but it does keep us moving forward at a nice clip. If we can agree life is more of a marathon than a sprint, then maybe a measured pace better fits the bill.

We know hovering is inefficient. There are hidden barriers to our endeavors. Knowing how to anticipate obstacles and take the necessary steps to move past them provides a huge payoff.

It's exactly the same with anything we attempt to accomplish in our lives:

- Staying where we are, regardless of the reason, WILL suck our resources.
- Making a plan and starting to execute it WILL uncover obstacles that must be overcome.
- Overcoming the obstacles WILL significantly increase the ease, motivation, sense of accomplishment and self-confidence needed to have a productive and fulfilling life.

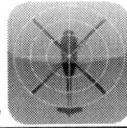

Hover *Check*

- What hover are you in right now?

- List the obstacles you will need to negotiate:

- List the payoffs once you accomplish your goal:

EMERGENCY PROCEDURE 3

IF IN A HOVER, ETL OR FORWARD FLIGHT: UNDERSTAND THE FOLLOWING:

✦ Staying in a hover WILL suck our resources: energy, time & money

✦ Making a plan & executing it WILL uncover obstacles that must be overcome

✦ Continuing through the obstacles WILL significantly increase the ease, motivation, sense of accomplishment & self-confidence needed to have a productive and fulfilling life

IMMEDIATELY DETERMINE THE TYPE OF "HOVER TRAP" YOU'VE ENCOUNTERED

TM 55-1520-237-CL   E-3

PART II

Hover Traps

Like the Bermuda Triangle, hover traps are mysterious, vexing behaviors making opportunities, potential, and accomplishment vanish, seemingly without a trace.

Photo II-1 A Blackhawk on final approach in brown out conditions.
(US Army photo by Bryanna Poulin)

If you're like me, you may have come to the conclusion it's not, "Me against the world," but rather "Me against me." We are often our own worst enemy. We waste time, energy, and opportunities because of habits we've developed slowly over time, bad habits we may not even know we have.

Hover Trap: *Term used to describe a person's or organization's actions, habits or beliefs that block positive progress; A habitual activity derailing one from their intended goal; Any behavior or activity keeping one busy but not effective.*

The goal of this section is to identify the worst of these traps, describe them and give them names. We've already learned a hover is inefficient and requires a lot of power, and that maximum endurance airspeed, although moderate in speed, does not use as much power and is optimum and sustainable for the long term.

Some of these traps will resonate with you; others will not. Since we're all different, complex people, we can fall into different combinations and degrees of these traps. There might be a trap I don't mention. (I would love to hear about it. My contact information is in the back of the book.) The important thing is to identify it, describe it, and name it. Only after we define a trap can we create a strategy to avoid it.

As you read about these traps, think about how they might apply to you. Try to identify what is keeping you busy but not effective. Remember, we are in the Truth Room.

CHAPTER 4

Rescue Mission

Hover Trap #1

"I can hear you, but can't see you," crackled the voice over the radio. Scanning the jagged grainy-green peaks through my goggles, ironically I too could hear but not see him.

"Romeo Lima, Rebel 16. Start your long count."

We received word just before dark. Two soldiers, conducting an early morning reconnaissance, got lost in the rugged mountains, ran out of water, and with the sun in descent the temperature had dropped. Their saving grace was that they had taken a radio with them and we knew their frequency.

Determined not to compromise the counter-narcotics operation we were supporting, we decided to launch an aircraft after dark. Armed with their known starting point, we plotted our search grid.

The Blackhawk is equipped with a capability called FM Homing. When selected, a needle in the cockpit locks on and points toward the transmitting FM frequency. If we happened to over fly them, the needle would swing 180 degrees. Using GPS, we should be able to locate them in short order, even at night.

"Rebel 16, you just flew over us."

Slowing the aircraft and making a 180, I asked for another long count.

"Roger, 10, 9, 8, 7...."

"Sir, I have them. At your one o'clock," The crew chief directed.

"Romeo Lima, we have you in sight."

They were perched on an outcropping above a very steep cliff at the apex of sharp ridge line. I circled to find a clearing to land. There wasn't one, but I had an idea and briefed the crew on what we would do.

With the parking brake set and sitting in the right seat, I inched the aircraft toward the cliff's ledge. The right main wheel was behind me, but right below the crew chief's position. He guided me in.

"Two feet forward, one foot down."

I made the corrections fixed on two reference points.

"Stop forward, one foot down, six inches..."

Feeling the right main wheel touch down, I reduced power just a hair more to create a pivot point, and reminded myself to breathe. With the rest of the aircraft still flying over the cliff, I felt the aircraft rock while the two men were pulled on board.

With an "All Secured" from the back, I lifted off and to the left, into the night. I transferred the controls to my co-pilot and hidden in the darkness of the cockpit exhaled a long breath.

Photo 4-1 A balancing act: With no place to land, this pilot is using the main wheel as a pivot point. (US Army photo by Staff Sgt. Aubree Clute)

There's a tried and true equation every aviator must know: Airspeed + Altitude = Options. The situation has deteriorated rapidly if a pilot runs out of all three at the same time. Options give us time to assess the situation and develop a plan for the best path forward. If we don't have time, we have to move on the issue immediately.

There's a tried and true equation every aviator must know: Airspeed + Altitude = Options!

When I'm interviewing a prospective client who's in career transition or contemplating a move, I always ask a very important, direct and, some might think, crass question: "How long do you have before your money runs out?"

I'm not asking to determine if my potential client has means to pay for my services. Although I'm sure some may think this is the case, I ask to determine if what we are facing is an urgent Rescue Mission instead of a strategic career management engagement.

It's another way of asking, "How much time do we have?" Knowing how much time is left before real catastrophe strikes is important and informs me as to what course of action we need to take. For example, what is the difference between these two answers?

- There is talk of some major changes coming down but it won't happen for at least two quarters.
- I've been out of work for 18 months and if I don't land something within the next month I may lose my house.

A sense of real urgency exists because time is the enemy in the second answer. If something doesn't happen fast, the situation will deteriorate more rapidly than it already has. Answer two has the makings of a Rescue Mission.

During a rescue mission, the main concern is addressing immediate needs now. Emergency procedures are immediate action steps required to save the crew and aircraft from going out of control.

We Ride Our Mistakes to the Ground

Unlike our jet-flying brethren, helicopter aviators can't eject from a stricken helicopter. Similarly, we can't eject out of our lives. Broken aircraft don't fix themselves in the air. They need to land. In the same way, situations in our lives don't fix themselves either. We need a purposeful plan to fix them. Ignore a Hover Trap at your own risk.

Sam: Don't Save Me

I regularly offer free consultations to prospective clients for two reasons. The first is fit. What I do is intensely personal. I want my clients to know I'm the right fit for them and vice versa. Secondly, and just as important, I need to know I can help them. If I think the situation is outside my area of expertise, I know many experts to whom I can refer them.

The worst scenario for me is when I can't convince a person I know I can help to grab the lifeline I'm offering. Sam was someone I knew I could help if he would just grab on. He was referred by a mutual friend. Sam needed a rescue mission.

I sat with Sam for what turned out to be two hours, listening and taking notes. He had already been unemployed for some time, and from what he was describing, was stuck and desperate. Or was he?

- He was behind on his mortgage, but his son was still on a traveling sports team.
- He wouldn't consider a temporary, part-time job, but drove to his second home for weekends.
- He admitted there was intense strain on his relationship with his wife over finances, but drove a nice SUV.
- He said he wanted to make something happen, but rebuffed any suggestion of modifying his lifestyle.

I only met him once for two hours and unfortunately we did not engage. Through the grapevine, I heard he lost his house and was living in his vacation home. Maybe that's what he really wanted all along. I don't know.

I do know this. Like balancing a helicopter on one wheel over a cliff, during a rescue mission you must be willing to take some out-of-the-box actions and time is of the essence.

Ask yourself: What is the most time-critical situation you need to address now? I know that when it comes to your family, friends, career, and health it's hard to pick just one area that's most important but if you sit and think about it, you will do so. If you are having trouble deciding, talk to a trusted friend and ask for advice. Fortunately, and sometimes unfortunately, it seems my friends live in the Truth Room too. (If you don't have anybody to talk to, we've just found another problem.)

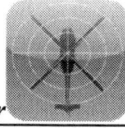

Hover *Check*

- Are you in a situation requiring a Rescue Mission?

- Conduct an asset inventory. List your physical and relationship assets here:

- Determine how much time you have in hours, days, weeks, or months before a significant, negative event will occur:

- List immediate actions you can take to stabilize the situation:

- Convene a War Council of your most trusted friends now.

EMERGENCY PROCEDURE 4

IF A SUDDEN AND SEVERE SITUATION OCCURS THAT IS ADVERSELY AFFECTING YOUR LIFE IMMEDIATELY:

+ Launch a rescue mission

+ Conduct an asset inventory

+ Determine how much time you have

+ Execute actions to stabilize the situation

+ Convene a War Council of your most trusted friends

NOTE: A RESCUE MISSION MEANS TIME IS OF THE ESSENCE – MOVE OUT!

TM 55-1520-237-CL   E-4

CHAPTER 5

I'm Too Special
(Nobody Will Understand)
Hover Trap #2

We filed into a small auditorium classroom with a chalkboard and lectern at the front. Forty of us, coming from the flight line, were grateful for the air conditioning. Summer in lower Alabama is hot and humid. Flight suits, still stained with sweat from our morning flying session, and rings around the ears from our flight helmet speakers gave the room a gymnasium feel.

Excitement was in the air. Our class had just finished the first phase of flight school: Primary. Next would be low-level navigation, instrument training, and transition to our combat aircraft. Then we would get tactical, cross-country, and night vision goggle training.

We all had months and months of training ahead of us, but we had completed phase one. We were all feeling good about ourselves.

A salty older man, dressed in street clothes, addressed the class. By salty, I mean this guy looked like he was held together by caffeine and nicotine. His weathered face was etched with furrows, no doubt from countless hours scanning instruments, terrain, and weather. Underneath bushy gray brows, his eyes were still sharp and precise. But it was his voice that I still remember over twenty years later. It was deep, calm, and commanding. I wanted to listen to him.

"Congratulations! You can fly. If a state of emergency existed, like it did during Vietnam, this would be the end of your training. You would graduate and we would ship you all out."

What? I thought, they wouldn't just throw us out there now, would they? We've been told we're the best of the best and the cream of the crop. It was so competitive just getting accepted to flight school.

One of my classmates spoke out authoritatively, "You couldn't do that. We haven't even had instrument training yet."

You are not that special! Does that come as a shock to you? It seems a little harsh, doesn't it? Well, it is.

Yeah, I thought, take that. Like spectators watching a tennis match, everybody's head turned in unison back toward the instructor.

"Oh *yes* we could!" came the barking retort. "We would give you a tactical weather endorsement and off you'd go. Of course, it would depend on the needs of the service."

Holy crap he's serious! I thought. Sure, we finished Primary but we were all still, well...dangerous.

He flipped the chalkboard over and listed in three columns the aircraft he had flown, from helicopters to airplanes. It looked like he had flown every type of aircraft the Army ever operated.

"I know a little bit about flying," he continued. "Look around you. If you spend a career in Army Aviation one out of every four of you will be dead. If you want to increase your odds of survival, listen to what I'm about to say." He paused, scanning the room for effect.

Suddenly it seemed a little cold. In about one minute I had gone from feeling like the cream of the crop to feeling very expendable. I listened.

Photo 5-1 *Feeling and looking special. The author was a flight Platoon Leader for 33 months before taking command of an Assualt Helicopter Company.(Via Author)*

Guess what? You are not *that* special either! Does that come as a shock to you? It seems a little harsh, doesn't it? Well, it is, and it's true...sort of.

The famous French aviator and novelist, Antoine de Saint-Exupéry, in his 1943 novella, *The Little Prince*, writes of a boy Prince that falls in love with a rose. The rose professes to be the only one of its kind in the entire world. Later in the story, the Prince finds a garden of 5,000 roses all looking like his and sadly reflects, *"I thought that I was rich, with a flower that was unique in all the world; and all I had was a common rose."* (Saint-Exupery, 1943)

How many times have we convinced ourselves or others of how special we are? Because we are so unique and special we should be afforded special privileges. We are experts at creating layers of façade to outwardly convince others of our ultimate specialness. Unfortunately, like the rose, we are either misinformed or delusional.

So too is anybody who thinks they are so unique that surely no one else could understand what they are going through or how to help them. The "I'm Too Special" hover trap occurs when we think nobody can help us so we tell ourselves, "What's the point in asking?" We stay stuck. Bad idea.

Although we are all self-absorbed and entitled, most of us do a good job of keeping these impulses in check. Usually, our societal norms respond to anybody behaving too badly, maintaining a kind of equilibrium. But things may be changing.

A recent study conducted by Sara Konrath, a researcher at the University of Michigan, compared the level of empathy of today's college students to college students 30 years ago, essentially their parents, and found surprising results. Konrath found today's college students are a full 40% less empathetic, earning the Gen Y/Millennials cohort the not-so-flattering moniker the "I Generation" or "Generation Me." (Smithstein, 2010) Konrath goes so far as to state it's a narcissism epidemic ignited, not by the Millennials, but by their later Boomer and Gen X'er parents. There is enough blame to go around.

The problem I have with this trend is that it may lead us to being less self-regulating, resilient, and well-rounded people. I fear that the traits most needed when our world is full of challenge, change and seemingly ever increasing chaos are exactly the skills we as a society are trending away from.

Taken to the extreme, this self-centered existence leads to isolation. In his book, *Malignant Self-Love*, Dr. Sam Vaknin examines traits of people who have slipped too far into a clinical narcissistic state. My proposition isn't that we are all narcissists, but read on and you'll see what I saw: alarming patterns of behavior, albeit extreme. Here's what I mean.

Vaknin notes a rejection of habit. (Vaknin, 2007) That is, feeling no need to follow routines or set procedures as part of a larger pattern of aggressive entitlement. Only doing what one likes, and only when one likes to do it, may be motivated by an over-exaggerated elevation of one's position. Whenever waiting in line, in traffic or just thinking it, we think we are above it and the rules don't apply to us.

Here is why you don't want to be too special. Vaknin states these, "feelings of supremacy often mask a cancerous inferiority complex." (Vaknin, 2007) This is important to know. Whether you, a family member, close friend, or colleague are struggling with this issue, it's the underlying insecurities you need to deal with.

Once we identify, confront, and establish a realistic, rational level of uniqueness, only then can we begin to change the dialogue from, "I'm so unique," to "How can I uniquely contribute?"

The truth is each of us is very unique and special while at the same time we are very much the same. It's a paradox worth spending some time on because it can stop us from accomplishing what is required to move successfully forward in any aspect of our lives.

Each one of us possesses personality, talents, perspectives, thought processes, and experiences that inform our personal and unique view of the world. Like our unique DNA, thumbprint, or iris pattern, this individuality is important to acknowledge and understand. We all bring something special to the party. Be it doing something common, uncommonly well or making something uncommon, seem commonplace. This is your value-add.

We all bring something special to the party. Be it doing something common, uncommonly well or making something uncommon, seem commonplace.

We should know our unique value-add and be able to articulate it first to ourselves and, just as importantly, to others. It's funny how some of the things we are great at we discount as near meaningless. I know I have done this. Have you?

For example I'm good at creating metaphors that support key learning points. This book is an example (I hope).

Now, take a few moments and think first about what aspects of your life you want to examine. For example, you may choose Career and the sub-aspect could be Sales. Then list your unique value-adds, what you can uniquely contribute. Don't stop at just one. Instead, use this time as a free-flowing thought exercise.

Here's an example:

🜚 Life Aspect: Career

- Sub-Aspect: Sales
- Unique Value-Add:
  - Ability to develop logical process connections and conceptualize them for a client.
  - Ability to see possibilities instead of only obstacles.
  - Ability to communicate abstract concepts in a way others can understand and apply.

On a separate sheet, do the same exercise for each of the five Hover Aspects (Family, Friends, Career, Health, and Spiritual) and fill out a long list of unique, value-added attributes. If you can't articulate them, ask a close friend, family member, mentor, or coach. Trust me; they know your value-add.

On a micro level, we are special and unique. We bring skills and capabilities that can enhance our relationships, friendships, organizations, and overall wellbeing. On a macro level the situation may be much different. Let's look at this scenario now.

As a pilot, zooming along at low level, climbing to clear trees and flicking the aircraft into a bank to fit between obstacles, I was aware of every detail flashing by me. The leaves on the trees, branches, fences, clearings, roads, power lines, even smells were all vivid and detailed. At 5,000 feet, however, things looked more homogeneous. Of course I could see roads, terrain features, fields, rivers, and lakes, but with no detail. It happens the same way when we take the macro view of some of our experiences.

A few years ago it hit home for me. Yes, I have always known I'm unique with talents special to me, but as I was reading a local newspaper showing the statistics of the town I lived in I didn't feel quite so special. It went something like this:

- Average house size: 1900 square feet. That's the size of my house.
- Average age of residents: 30. That's how old I am (at the time).
- Marital Status: Married. Hey, I'm married.
- Education: High School or higher 95%. Check.
- Average commute to work: 30 minutes. Yes.

I'm not feeling very unique and special anymore. In fact, I'm starting to feel downright average. But it gets even better:

- Prostate cancer is the most common cancer (excluding skin cancer) among American men. So I have that to look forward to.
- The hair on the top of my head is thinning, but I have a never-ending supply growing from my ears.
- My belts are getting longer but my memory is getting shorter.
- Studies show that the average working American will have three to five careers and between 10 to 12 jobs during his or her lifetime.

I could go on, but I think you get the point. As an individual, are you unique and special? Yes. Are you an anomaly in the Third standard deviation? I don't think so.

In fact, I challenge you to think of the most demanding interpersonal issue you have ever faced, and I'm convinced many people have had the same or worse issue. Think of the worst medical condition you have ever been confronted with and I will find many more that share your same diagnosis, then find others with ones that are worse.

Examine all the life aspects we've been talking about in this book. Yes, others have been there and worse. Most importantly, many have survived, overcome and thrived.

Don't get me wrong. My aim is not to minimize your tough situations and whitewash them as insignificant. They are significant.

My main points are:

- ⵯ Although it often feels we are uniquely challenged by our personal obstacles, we 100% are not.
- ⵯ There are others who have been through the same fire and triumphed.

We should gather strength from this fact, seek out advice, and dedicate all our energy to getting out of our current situation. Beyond the hover of our current situation, there is clean air.

Interestingly, many of us, knowingly or otherwise, invest huge amounts of time and effort in the design and creation of the same custom-made gilded cage we so often bitterly rail against.

Just like with ETL, once we've out-flown our own vortices, we will require less energy to move forward and accomplish our goals. It is up to us to initiate the movement toward the solution.

Adversity is not the exception in life, it is the rule. True character is measured by how we address our personal adversity. Finding the right landing zone on a sunny day does not test the professionalism of an aircraft crew. Accomplishing the mission at night with goggles, during rain squalls and high winds, does.

As I have mentioned before, we are most often the ones constructing limitations around our capabilities, severely hampering our potential. Yes, we are the general contractors who built the box confining our lives and the pilots who allow our helicopters to hover and burn precious fuel, wasting our limited time and energy. It seems we would rather be busy and stuck than effective and making progress.

Interestingly, many of us, knowingly or otherwise, invest huge amounts of time and effort into the design and creation of the same custom-made, gilded cages we often bitterly rail against. In this sense we are all uniquely the same.

Hover *Check*

🕊 Take a moment to reflect on how you are unique from others and write your thoughts down.

🕊 Now think about all you have in common with humanity and write that down. (Try to get beyond: two feet, two hands, etc., and think about common threads of our human existence, i.e.: loss, fear, love, etc.)

EMERGENCY PROCEDURE 5

IF YOU THINK YOU ARE <u>SO SPECIAL</u> THAT NOBODY CAN RELATE TO YOUR PROBLEMS <u>IMMEDIATELY</u>:

- Get over yourself

- Know others have experienced what you are experiencing (and worse)

- Ensure you don't lose perspective

- Seek out advice from your trusted advisor

- Know doing nothing is very costly

CHAPTER 6

I Can Change by Myself
Hover Trap #3

During WWI, aerial combat was born as an individual sport. Roland Garros, Max Immelmann, Oswald Boelcke, Lanoe Hawker, and Manfred von Richthofen largely worked alone. As aircraft increased in speed and capability, the need for defined tactics, maneuvers, and teamwork became increasingly important to the survival of combat aviators. The increased complexity and lethality of aerial combat transformed from an individual to a team sport.

By the beginning of WWII, propeller-driven aircraft were already approaching their aerodynamic limits. There was still much work to be done in developing tactics to minimize an enemy's strength while maximizing one's own.

A perfect example of this requirement came during the United States' early involvement in WWII. Naval aviator John "Jim" Thach

Photo 6-1 LCDR John "Jim" S. Thach.
(Courtesy of the US National Archives)

realized the heavier American fighters could not turn as tight as the lighter, more maneuverable Japanese fighter aircraft, especially the venerable Mitsubishi A6M Zero-Sen.

Late in 1941, Thach invented a maneuver he called the Beam Defense Position, which came to be called the Thach Weave.

This maneuver is so elegant in that it is at once defensive and offensive. While requiring tremendous teamwork, it also negates the inherent strength of the opponent. I have illustrated the Thach Weave using a two-aircraft element but it can be scaled to a four-aircraft section and larger formations.

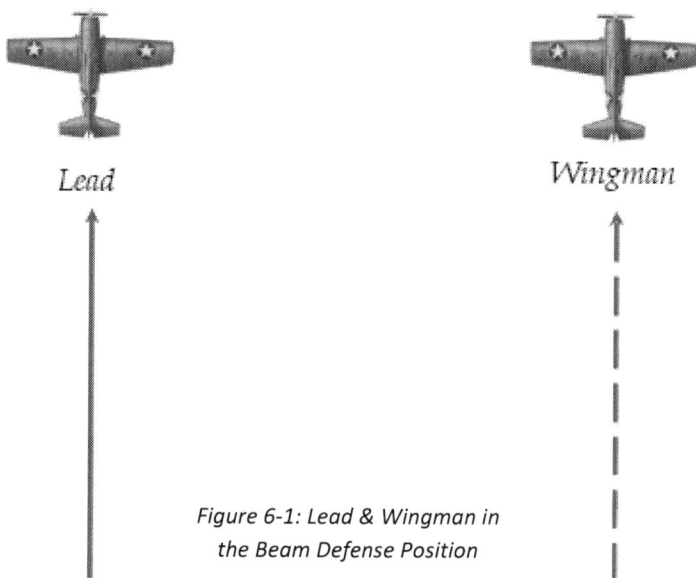

Lead   *Wingman*

Figure 6-1: Lead & Wingman in the Beam Defense Position

Each element has a designated Lead pilot and Wingman. They fly abeam of each other. Both are continuously scanning the sky for intruders. In aerial combat, the odds greatly favor the side that first sees their opponent.

Figure 6-2 depicts the sudden appearance of an aggressor making an attack on the Lead aircraft.

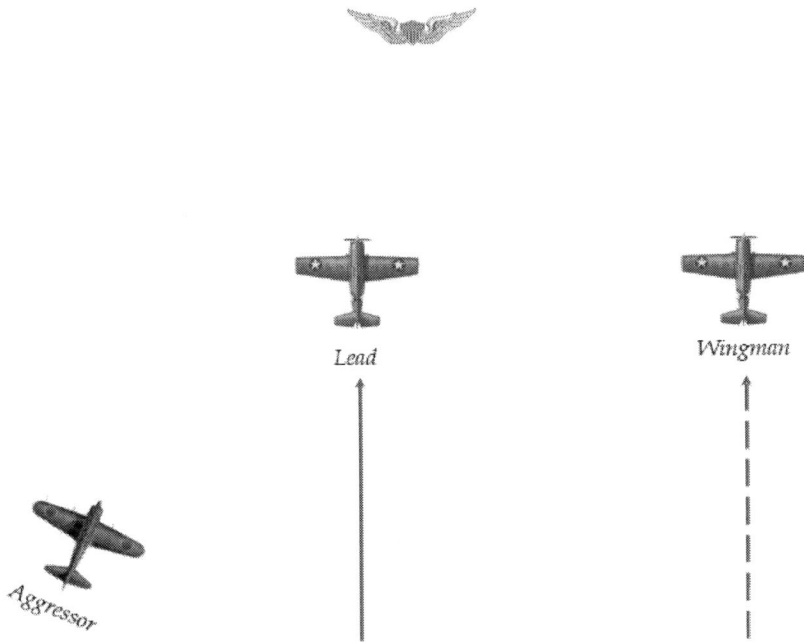

Figure 6-2: Aggressor attempts to attack the Lead Aircraft

Alerted to the new danger, Figure 6-3 shows Lead and Wingman aggressively turn into each other; Lead, in a defensive move, but also to drag the aggressor in front of the Wingman. The Wingman turns into the aggressor and is now in the best position to protect the Lead.

History proved its effectiveness, even against more agile opponents. It can work for you too.

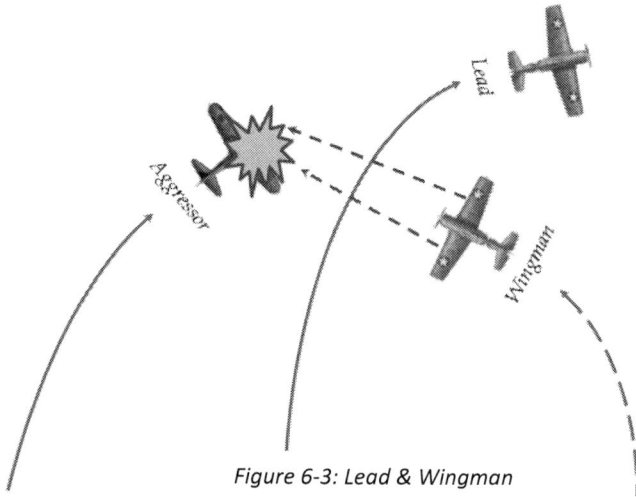

Figure 6-3: Lead & Wingman turn toward each other putting the Wingman into firing position

After dispatching the aggressor, Figure 6-4 depicts the Lead and Wingman returning to the Beam Defense Position, ready to execute the maneuver again if required. This can be done as many times as required and history has proven it effective even against more agile opponents. It can work for you too.

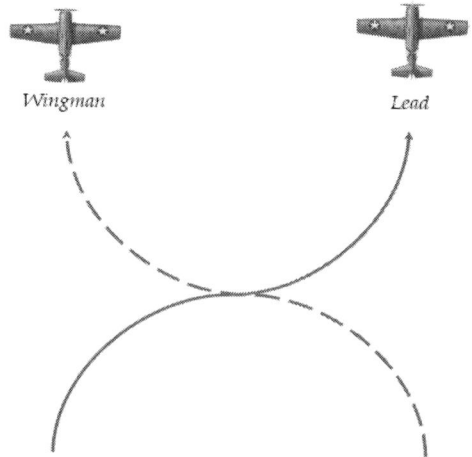

Figure 6-4: Lead & Wingman regain "Beam Defense Position" ready to execute the maneuver again, if necessary

> *"Habit is habit, and not to be flung out of the window by any man, but coaxed downstairs a step at a time."*
>
> *- Mark Twain*

Now, what if we have a habit (or habits) stopping us from being successful with our family, relationships, career or health? Would we appreciate a little help in overcoming it? Wouldn't it be incredible if we each had somebody watching out for us, constantly scanning for danger, and ready to pounce, guns blazing, onto anybody or anything that was not in our best interest?

Like success in aerial combat, I'm 100% convinced success in life (enter your definition here) is also a team sport and for a lot of the same reasons: aggressors, complexity, and endurance.

Habits are complex, insidious actions that, if allowed, have the power to propel us forward or hold us back. However, not all are bad. Remember, there are good habits, too. It's worth taking a closer look at:

- The dynamics of habits.
- Why we repeatedly attempt change alone?
- The role of the trusted advisor.

Let's start with a definition: *"Habits are behaviors that are performed automatically because they have been performed frequently in the past. This repetition creates a mental association between the situation (cue) and action (behavior) which means when the cue is encountered the behavior is performed automatically. Automaticity has a number of components, one of which is lack of thought."* (Lally, 2009)

Using this definition, getting repeatedly stuck in a hover trap could be a habit initiated by a certain set of circumstances, including your environment. For example, if you are prone to freeze when presented with opposition and are not moving forward or back but vacillating on a course of action, it may be a habit you can overcome. There could be other reasons this is happening, but habit is one of the most important.

The Dynamics of Habits

Armed with this definition, habits, especially the disruptive ones, are something we do automatically, without conscious thought, over and over again. It might take an outsider to alert us to our habits.

I remember recently creating a video for my website. It was done in an interview style with me answering questions from somebody off screen. When I received the first edit, I realized I reached up and touched my nose while I was talking. It was very distracting to me. I asked my wife to watch the video and tell me what she thought. She noticed the nose grab also and added, "You do that all the time." I had no idea I had that particular habit until I saw it on video. One call to the videographer and the nose grab disappeared forever. Wouldn't it be great if all bad habits could be banished as easily?

One of the most important dynamics of habits is that they are difficult for us to detect on our own. First we must realize that much of what we do is based on habits. Then it's important to create a mechanism to identify all our habits, both good and bad. We want to obviously reinforce the good habits and keep them going.

> *We all have idiosyncrasies and, let's face it, that's what makes people so interesting.*

The habits that precipitate hovering, however, are those we need to eliminate. We need to understand what cues and behaviors drive these habits and develop a plan to make the appropriate changes. That sounds easy. But if it truly was easy, all of us would have no vices or bad habits and we would be the most productive and successful people we know.

I'm not an advocate of changing everything about everybody all at once. We all have idiosyncrasies and, let's face it, that's what makes people so interesting. I do, however, think focusing on one area of improvement is the most effective.

Habits are situational. They are connected to a context and in many ways are subconscious conditioned responses. Take a moment to think about what specific habit is holding you back the most. Write it down. We will use it later.

Say you want to lose weight and be more health conscious. If you still hang out with a group of people who smoke, eat unhealthy food, and don't exercise, your chances for positive change are minimal. "Breaking habits is very difficult. The easiest way is to control your environment so you do not encounter the cue which triggers your habit. It is difficult to break any habit even when you are motivated to do so. If you are ambivalent about breaking it then you will be less likely to succeed." (Lally, 2009)

Our work is cut out for us. On average it takes 66 days to form a new habit, according to Phillippa Lally in a study published in the *European Journal of Social Psychology*. This gives us insight into how long it will take to get rid of an existing, unwanted one.

Why We Repeatedly Attempt Change Alone

It's all about us. For Americans, the term rugged individualism has been ingrained into our identities. Often, like a habit, we don't realize it's there. Ask the rest of the world and they will tell you Americans are different.

In a *Time* magazine article, Roger Rosenblatt said it like this, "The 'rugged' saves 'rugged individualism' from shabbiness by implying not merely solitary but courageous action....Davy Crockett, Thomas Edison, Teddy Roosevelt, Henry Ford. Those fellows built a nation with their hands." (Rosenblatt, 1984) If they can do it, so can I, by myself!

It is one of the enigmas of human frailty that allows us to continue to think, in every circumstance, we alone can solve our own problems.

Gary Ryan Blair in his 100-day Challenge states, "Self-reliance is all about freedom from the control or influence of outside parties...the choices, after all, are yours. You choose happiness. You choose sadness. You choose decisiveness. You choose ambivalence. You choose success. You choose failure. You choose courage. You choose fear." (Blair, 2010)

And I don't think this self-contained personal ethos is exclusive to Americans. Anyone who has risked much and gained much has earned membership in the self-reliant club. In every corner of this earth, there are people who fit this profile. In a way, I think everybody has a little of it in them. It is one of the enigmas of human frailty that allows us to continue to think, in every circumstance, we alone can solve our own problems.

Even the most macho fighter pilot will ask for help, usually right before he reaches between his legs to pull the black and yellow ejection handles.

The Role of the Trusted Advisor: Your Wingman

Like the Wingman in the beginning of this chapter, we can all benefit from having an objective advisor in our corner, someone who has our best interests in mind. Everybody should have a trusted wingman. They go by different names: Friend, Mentor, Advisor, Coach or Wingman. It doesn't matter the name, the function is what's important.

Why do the most talented among us have coaches while others don't? The best atheletes have coaches not to create talent but to enhance, challenge, and optimize it. A trusted advisor shouldn't change us, instead they should help us become *MORE* of who we are.

What is more important in our lives than our family, friends, careers, health, and spiritual well-being? With our world becoming more complex and competitive, we all need somebody to help us stay on track, focused on difficult but important tasks, who also challenges us to be our best selves. A trusted advisor or Wingman can do that for you. They can see when you're stalled in a busy mode and nudge you out of it.

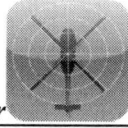

Hover _Check_

✦ Think about a time when you sorely missed having a trusted advisor or wingman to support you. Write it down.

✦ Make a list of likely wingmen who meet the following criteria:
   1. Has your best interests in mind
   2. Has your trust and confidence
   3. Will tell you what you need to hear
   4. Challenges you to be your best
   5. Listens, understands, and delivers what you need
   6. Is a partner in your success
      a.
      b.
      c.
      d.
      e.

✦ Contact them. Have a quality discussion with them. Explain what you're planning and how they can help.

✦ Consistency is important. Ask them for the commitment to be with you until your issue is resolved.

EMERGENCY PROCEDURE 6

IF IT SEEMS YOU ARE CONSTANTLY DUELING WITH MORE AGILE OPPONENTS IN YOUR LIFE IMMEDIATELY SEEK OUT A WINGMAN WHO WILL:

- Have your best interests in mind

- Tell you what you need to hear not what you want to hear

- Challenge you to be your best

- Listen and deliver what you need

- Be a partner in your success

TM 55-1520-237-CL   E-6

CHAPTER 7

Who's Your Wingman?
Hover Trap #4

Tell me with whom thou art found, and I will tell thee who thou art.
- Johann Wolfgang von Goethe (1749-1832)

Still ringing true over 400 years later, I mention this well-worn saying for a very good reason. Often, whom we associate with is a significant part of our hovering problem. While it's not always the case, it's so fundamental and can be so counter-productive I have to mention it.

The experience of the Officer Basic Course and Flight School at Fort Rucker, Alabama, was a life game-changer for me. I came from a small, private university where I felt I was a big fish in a small pond. Probably like many, I drove onto the base full of youthful hubris. As a newly minted lieutenant, I *was* somebody special.

Why shouldn't I think so? I had passed the flight aptitude test and the flight physical. I was assessed in the top 10% of all incoming lieutenants entering the Army that year, and was the number-one cadet in my ROTC battalion, even winning the George C.

> *"What are you going to do, Lieutenant?!"*

Marshall Leadership Award where the winners were flown to the Virginia Military Institute to meet the Chief of Staff of the

Army. Move over, Tom Cruise—I'm your new Top Gun replacement.

Decades later, I can still remember the feeling of anticipation and excitement reserved especially for the young. I also remember the feeling of almost panic when I met the rest of my flight class.

They were all the number one cadets from their schools. They all played varsity sports and they all seemed just a little smarter than me. I was both excited to be considered one of them and at the same time intimidated that they were my peers. I was now a small fish in a very large pond.

I found myself thinking about what my instructors used to always ask us, "What are *you* going to do, Lieutenant?!"

Photo 7-1 Flight Class 89-07, 2LT Gryske is first row third from left. (Via author)

In flight school, I was surrounded by a group of highly motivated, smart, focused men and women. It was a challenge to keep up with them. Unfortunately, everybody doesn't have such a positive peer group. One's social group, family, or friends have a significant impact on how and if we can be successful at making a significant change in our lives and fly out of the hover into the clean air. Be careful, because it's a double-edged sword that can easily cut both ways.

Here are some examples of peer groups making a negative impact. Recognizing that there are significant medical issues involved, if a recovering drug addict comes out of rehab clean only to rejoin her old group of friends, what do you think the outcome will be? Failure, and back in her hover, more discouraged than before. Drug relapse is 40% - 60%. (McLellan AT, 2000)

For criminals, recidivism within three years of release is 67%. (Gibbons JJ, 2006) That means nearly 7 of every 10 prisoners released are rearrested within three years and 52% of those are re-incarcerated. How important do you think it is to make a new life with new associations after leaving prison? The same dynamics occur in our lives when we are trying to accomplish something new and better, not the same old thing.

If you're reading this book because you're searching for something better than what you have right now—be it new capabilities, a rejuvenated career, relationships or life direction— think about WHO you are associating with.

If your social network is holding you back and doesn't support your new direction, what are your chances for long-term success? This is the cutting both ways I alluded to. Unfortunately, this could mean a family member or spouse is an obstacle you will need to adroitly negotiate. Identifying and addressing these relationships could be extremely difficult, but essential for you to be successful.

By the way, our associates don't have to be people. They could very well be old, negative tapes playing in our heads from long ago, possibly pushed aside from childhood. They could be the memory of a painful past failure or misstep that had lasting consequences. Today, it is very common for successful, middle-aged adults to come face to face with these potentially limiting, life-crushing companions, because they are just too burdensome to travel with anymore.

There's an upside, too! We live in the information age. Vast amounts of knowledge and networks of people are at our fingertips instantly. If we want to improve any aspect of our behaviors or our future direction, we can do so. With social networks ever evolving, one can easily find groups of like-minded individuals with whom to form new associations, associations that support the direction you're heading now, not taking you back to your old stomping grounds, but toward the future you want to create for yourself.

Matt: Making a Break for It

Matt had been a very successful executive in technology sales. At one point, his efforts produced the lion's share of his company's revenue with all the perks, privileges, and access to the key executives that success often brings. That all changed when his company was bought out by a much larger, more bureaucratic one. It didn't take long before Matt found himself stuck layers below key corporate leadership with no influence on or visibility to strategic decisions.

"After the merger, I felt I had been put in a little box and placed in the basement. It was very discouraging. I kind of retreated from view and just concentrated on my job. Management wasn't asking a lot of me, so over time I just slipped into a status quo mode. With most of my high-level contacts gone I concentrated on crafting deals and managing my new boss; not a bad guy, just not very much of a forward thinker.

"It was about two years after the merger when I really started to feel the passion was drying up. My boss effectively controlled my access to upper management and the creativity, which I think I thrived on, was gone. It was also about this time I decided I either needed to look for another opportunity or turn things around inside my organization.

"To be honest, I knew I had been underperforming to my potential and had just settled for being comfortable. I finally decided to make a plan to re-launch myself inside my organization. I made two lists: Things I'd Start Doing and Things I'd Stop Doing.

"I started connecting with my old executive team who were mostly still in the same industry. I started introducing myself to the new executive team and started proposing strategies to improve revenue within my segment. I started teaming with other internal organizations to collaborate on sales initiatives. I also started to work on myself by watching what I ate and exercising more.

"I stopped things that were time wasters. I chose to stop having, if not a bad attitude, a complacent attitude, and things started changing for me. I guess I started to care again. I'm a big planner and worked on how I wanted my future to look three years down the road. Using that plan, I made a pretty distinct break from the direction I was headed in and started heading toward where I wanted to be.

"It was the right choice for me. I was recently asked to create a strategic sales plan for my market segment and, through meetings with the executive team, have been invited to contribute to the execution of it on a company basis."

Matt realized he needed to leave his old habits behind and join a new network to obtain the career satisfaction and success he wanted. Brian Tracy, an internationally known author, speaker, and corporate training expert, broached the idea that, indeed, success leaves tracks. (Tracy, 2008)

Successful people identify the obstacles, make a plan, and do the things they need to do to accomplish their objectives. If you want to be better in your field, relationships, health, etc., find a Wingman today! Find somebody who has already done what you want to accomplish. Research it. Do the work! Do what

> *The act of change is like rewriting the future while making your past, history.*

they did. You will soon grow into your own and be out of the hover. The act of change is like rewriting the future while making your past, history.

Hover Check

✦ Is your social group holding you back? Helping you?

✦ If you are being held back, what are you going to do about it and by when?

✦ If a family member is creating an obstacle, what are you going to do about it and by when?

EMERGENCY PROCEDURE 7

IF YOUR SOCIAL GROUP IS AN
OBSTACLE TO YOUR SUCCESS
<u>IMMEDIATELY</u>:

+ Ask for support OR

+ Change it

IF YOUR FAMILY OR FAMILY MEMBER IS
AN OBSTACLE TO YOUR SUCCESS
<u>IMMEDIATELY</u>:

+ Deal with it directly AND

+ Ask for support

TM 55-1520-237-CL   E-7

CHAPTER 8

I'll Just Work Harder

Hover Trap #5

Instantly, I realized I'd done the wrong thing. I didn't have time to talk. Reducing power and diving forward was our only option, but did I react in time? I knew the Howitzer slung from the cargo hook was getting close to the ground. The aircraft shuddered and abruptly stopped descending while we picked up speed. Our descent did stop in time, but only just.

I was leading a two-ship mission to conduct what's called an artillery raid, a tactic involving quickly moving artillery pieces to a forward location, rapidly setting up, and firing at a predetermined target. Once completed, the aircraft would pick up the crew and guns and fly them back to their base.

Photo 8-1 UH-60A Blackhawk with a 105 Howitzer slung underneath. Capable of lifting the gun, gun crew and ammunition, the cargo hook could carry 8000 lbs. (Courtesy US Army)

While waiting for clearance to fly the last few kilometers, both aircraft slowed and finally stopped in a high hover. That was the mistake.

A helicopter in a high hover can be susceptible to a condition called Settling with Power or, the more technical term, Vortex Ring State. Settling with Power is a condition where the helicopter settles in its own downwash. *(FM 1-203 Fundamentals of Flight, Dept of Army, HQ, 1983)*

It can occur when a helicopter inadvertently starts to descend at a rate above 300 feet per minute (fpm) in a near vertical path. A 300-foot-per-minute rate of descent is not very fast and, at a high hover, it's more difficult for a pilot to notice the descent.

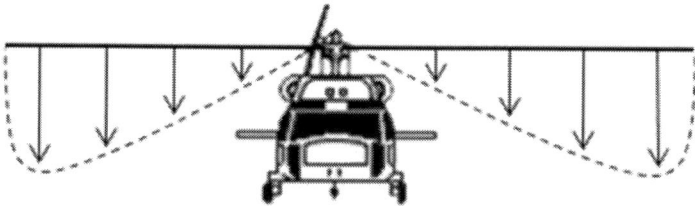

Figure 8-1 Air velocity in a stable hover

Stay with me here, because it will all come back to how we often react to situations, especially when faced with a large challenge. Figure 8-1 illustrates the velocity of the air flowing through the rotor system in a stable hover. The reason the downward lines are longer toward the outer tips of the rotor blades is because the tips are moving faster than the area of the blade closer to the rotor hub.

As the helicopter starts to descend, the air flow changes. Closer to the rotor hub, air is actually passing through the rotor system from the bottom, while the outer sections of the rotor are still pushing air down. Figure 8-2 shows this change in air flow pattern.

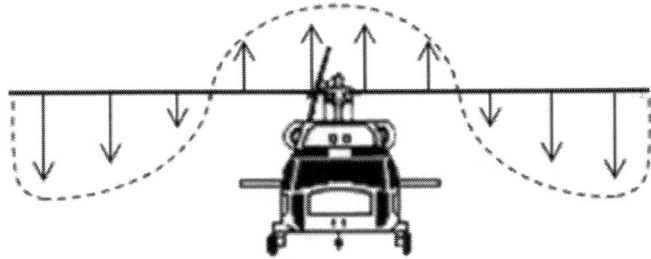

Figure 8-2 Conditions for Settling with Power developing

Here's the kicker we've been waiting for. If the pilot doesn't immediately identify the situation and correct it, Settling with Power will occur. Besides the vortices that always exist at the tips of the rotor blades, other vortices develop closer to the rotor hub. This robs the rotor system of critical lift capability.

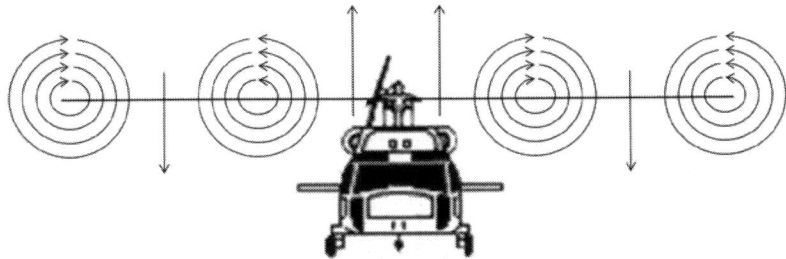

Figure 8-3 Air flow while Settling with Power

The clincher here is when the pilot finally does realize the situation he instinctively increases power to arrest the descent. This only increases the size of the vortices and the rate of descent. Figure 8-3 depicts a helicopter in trouble in a Settling with Power or Vortex Ring State condition.

With very little or no forward airspeed, the aircraft and the pilot will quickly run out of options. The more power they apply the more quickly they descend. Eventually, and unfortunately, we run out of four critical things all at once: Airspeed, Altitude, Power and Ideas. Yes, eventually there will be a crash.

⚜ How many times have you found yourself in this situation in your personal or professional life?

The "I'll just work harder trap" takes a tremendous toll on very capable people. The insidious nature of this trap sucks in some of the finest and brightest people in every kind of organization and leads them right to burn out when they least expect it. In a way it's the classic Busy vs. Effective scenario.

Chronic fatigue has pushed aside the allure of promotion, success, and money.

Highly motivated and dedicated individuals play right into its hands. If this has ever happened to you, you know exactly what I mean, and I doubt you will ever fall for it again. The scenario looks like this: You have a big client or project and things start to get a little sideways. No problem, you will just come in early to call the east coast and get things coordinated for the week. Soon, you are in early every day and the fires don't seem to go out until well after five. You cut out your morning workouts and your walks at lunch. You react by adding power.

Hey, it's just a bad week; you can hang, right? Your boss sees you working so hard and is impressed. He throws a special project your way for greater visibility with upper management, which is exactly what you want! You just wish you had time to put your best foot forward. You consistently stay later knowing deep down all this work will, one day, hopefully soon, pay off. You dig deep and add some more power.

There's no more power to apply.

You are now locked onto the prize and your bad week has turned into a blur of months and then quarters. You check your bag at the counter and the bags under your eyes as you get ready for yet another business trip. At this point, you realize you are rapidly running out of energy and power. Your productivity has slowed considerably. You used to get work done on the plane and now you're asleep before takeoff.

There's no more power to apply. You have reached a state of chronic fatigue, which has pushed aside the allure of promotion, success, and money. All is not lost, however. There is a way to get out of Settling with Power and the "I'll just work harder" hover trap.

One of the most professional officers I ever knew, James Arndt, trained me how to escape this condition. By intentionally inducing and recovering from Settling with Power, he ingrained in me a healthy respect for this type of situation while not being afraid of it.

Getting out of this trap is a powerful metaphor for when situations in life start to freefall regardless of how much effort we put into them. The immediate actions are counterintuitive but effective in arresting the descent and eliminating the danger. The results are so sudden it feels similar to reaching the ground floor in an elevator, a solid and sudden stop.

The results are so sudden it feels similar to reaching the ground floor in an elevator, a solid and sudden stop.

The pilot must reduce power and dip the nose of the helicopter to get it moving forward; flying out of the hover. This action resets the disturbed airflow in the rotor system. Figuratively, this could work for you, too.

Photo 8-2 Reducing power and pushing the nose down is counterintuitive but effective when recovering from Settling with Power. (Via author)

When we're caught in this hover trap in our professional or private lives, we have to metaphorically do the following things:

- Recognize we're in the trap.
- Realize that no matter how much effort we apply, doing more of the same will only make the situation worse.
- Disengage and view the problem from a new perspective.
- Implement a different approach to the problem, project, relationship, etc.

By changing our perspective, we will, in effect, reset the airflow and once again have the energy available to be positive, effective and creative. This is easier said than done. It may take asking a colleague, mentor, boss, or coach to assess the situation. Many of us might consider asking for help a sign of incompetence or weakness. But what's weaker: going down with the ship or solving the problem?

Linda: Work Became My Life

Linda had an established career in operations at a Fortune 500 company. She was known for delivering exceptional work on time, every time. Proud of her reputation and the esteem it garnered from her colleagues, she vowed to protect it at all costs. She just didn't know it would cost so much.

"I have always been a driven person. I like being a clutch player and having others depend on me. It gives me a great sense of satisfaction and pride. When I first heard the concept of Settling with Power, it went against what I believed in.

"In my experience, when something wasn't working out, I would just pour the coals on and bust through the issue. It worked for me for years. I gained a great reputation as being a 'go-to' person and it opened up opportunities for me, too."

This trap slowly draws in its victims by allowing their drive to lead to initial success. Like Linda, many become susceptible by developing habits that support this behavior. Leaders must be able to see this pattern developing in their subordinates and most importantly, within themselves.

"Over time, work slowly started to take over parts of my life. Friends, family, and even work suffered. I needed to start doing things differently and in a more sustainable way. The idea of initiating a reset now makes a lot of sense to me. I'm in that process now and see a lot of new opportunities to do things differently."

The Settling with Power metaphor was exactly what Linda needed to hear. The question now is, "Are you listening?"

On the following page, in Figure 8-4, I've included the Franklyn Covey Time Management Matrix. (Covey, 1995) It very simply and succinctly separates unimportant and important as well as urgent and non-urgent tasks. It's so time-tested and effective I thought, "Why re-invent the wheel?" But for it to work, we have to actually use it!

Notice how Important does not equal Urgent and Not Important does not equal Not Urgent. Important tasks are those that must be completed, period. Important tasks are not time bound. A kick-off meeting for a six-month project is Not Urgent, but very important to the success of the project.

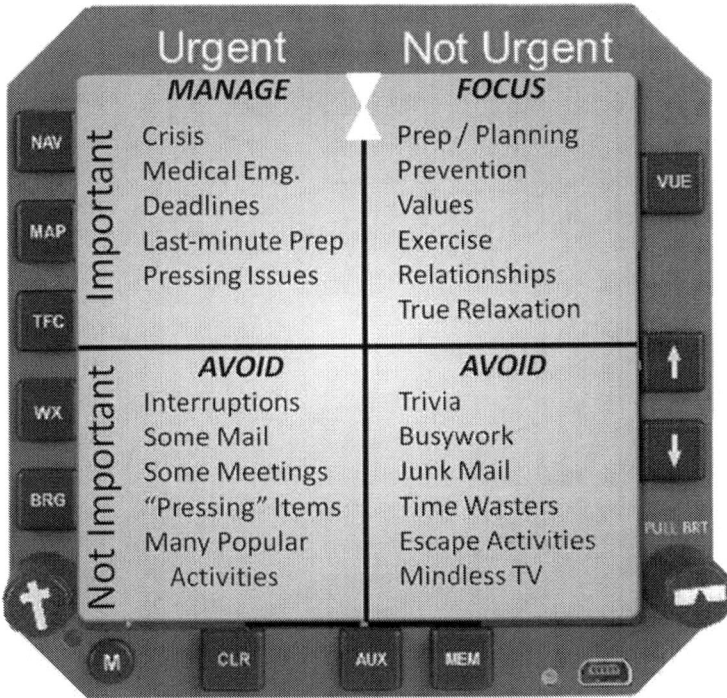

*Figure 8-4: Hover Trap Style: Franklyn Covey
Time Management Matrix* (Covey, 1995)

Urgency has to do with time and perceived due dates. However, the urgency of a task or issue has no bearing on its importance. It's up to us to manage the important and urgent items we need to take care of as well as focus on the important but not urgent tasks, such as planning.

Other hover traps can lead to this one, so always be on the lookout. Once it has us in its grip we must take quick and often counterintuitive actions to escape from it.

Hover Check

✦ Are you stuck in the, "I'll just work harder" hover trap?

✦ Review Figure 8-4. Make two lists. The first list should include the Important and Urgent tasks you must accomplish:

✦ Now list your Important and Non-Urgent tasks:

Congratulations! All remaining tasks should be delegated whenever possible.

EMERGENCY PROCEDURE 8

IF YOU ARE <u>EXHAUSTED</u> FROM USING ALL YOUR <u>ENERGY</u> & <u>POWER</u> BUT ARE STILL "DESCENDING." YOU ARE IN A <u>SETTLING WITH POWER</u> CONDITION.

<u>IMMEDIATELY</u> REDUCE POWER & GAIN AIRSPEED BY:

✈ First: Separate important from non-important tasks

✈ Second: List and manage your important & urgent tasks

✈ Third: List and focus on your important & non-urgent tasks

✈ Fourth: Complete the "nice to haves" only when time permits

✈ Continue your mission

TM 55-1520-237-CL   E-8

CHAPTER 9

Nothing's Wrong
Hover Trap #6

Looking through the goggles, I could see every detail, the formation lights, the glow of flame from the turbine engines, and every small movement of the aircraft in front and 30 degrees to our left. "Night vision goggles are amazing," I thought.

On a clear night with a full moon, it was not uncommon to fly as though it was broad daylight. The goggles allowed us to even see the shadows caused by the moonlight. (Answering the question I never thought to ask: Does a shadow exist if nobody can see it? With goggles, the answer is yes.)

Goggles are incredible technology but they also have limitations. Your field of view is limited to 40 degrees compared to our normal field of view of about 170 degrees. Visual acuity is at best 20/40 vision compared to our required 20/20 vision.

Another limitation was when landing at night in dusty conditions all you could see was what's best described as green static on a television. We called this a brown out.

A brown out occurs when the dust kicked up by the rotors obscures all vision from inside the aircraft. With no reference to guide the pilot, it is very easy to pick up considerable movement in any direction: sideways, forward, or even backward. Do this in a formation close to the ground and it's a recipe for disaster.

Because of the dusty conditions, the crew chief would report where the dust cloud caused by our rotor wash was in relation to our helicopter. I called out the altitude from our radar altimeter.

Photo 9-1 A Blackhawk about to be engulfed in a brown out caused by the downwash of the rotor blades. (Courtesy US Army)

The crew chief would call the position of the dust cloud as we touched down.

Clearing the trees, we flared to land.

"40 feet."

"Clouds at the tail."

"30 feet."

"Doors."

The aircraft shuddered as it came out of effective translational lift.

"20."

"Windows."

"10."

There was a hard bump. The tail wheel hit the ground, followed by the mains as the cockpit was engulfed in a cloud of dust. We were safely on the ground.

Timing is critical in these conditions. If the pilot hesitates while committing to plant the main wheels, you will be engulfed in a brown out. The standard procedures if this occurs are to simply pull power, level the wings, and initiate an immediate takeoff. Picking up speed and gaining altitude, we would exit the cloud and be able to see again.

I encountered brown outs many times in my flying career but only once did it almost lead to disaster. As a new copilot, we were landing under goggles and everything was going as planned except the cloud caught us before the main gear was on the ground. I felt the tail wheel bounce a few times. I could only see the swirl around us. The pilot flying made some corrections and reduced power instead of executing a go-around.

During what seemed like minutes but was more likely a couple of seconds, we picked up a drift to the left. When the left main gear hit the ground, we rolled up onto it and I braced for the main rotors striking the ground. I was sure we were going to roll over. Instead, in our cocoon of dust, the aircraft paused and slammed back down on all three wheels. We were lucky that night. All we did was scare ourselves to death.

As you can imagine, groping for the ground while in a disorienting environment can lead to disaster in aviation AND in our lives. What surprised me the most was how quickly I went from everything being under control to almost instantly being controlled by my circumstances.

When we don't realize something significant has changed, we can only react and wonder why the situation seems so difficult. What changed in my example? We lost sight of the ground and all visual references outside of the helicopter. What did we do wrong? We continued to try and land the aircraft as though we could see the ground, as though nothing was wrong.

It's just as important once we realize the situation has changed to do something about it. Since these topics are related, we will explore them here.

How many of us have done the exact same thing in our lives that my pilot and I did in the brown-out? Worse yet, how many of us are doing it now and don't realize it? Sometimes we're so busy hitting the wall we don't notice how futile our actions are.

In his special way, Dr. Spencer Johnson in his book *Who Moved My Cheese?* (Johnson, 2002), gently convicts us with his character, Hem. If you recall, Hem never left the cheese station, even after there was no more cheese. Even after he understood a significant negative change had occurred, he stayed, waiting for the situation to change instead of changing his situation.

So the "Nothing's Wrong" trap isn't about you not understanding things have changed, it's about you pretending and ACTING like nothing has changed. You know you're stuck busily hovering, but don't do anything to move forward.

In this situation, we freely admit there is a problem, but are unwilling or unable to formulate a coherent plan to tackle it. In essence, we are blindly stumbling around for the answer, hoping it will just appear. People do get lucky once in a while but most find this path a waste of both energy and, more importantly, time.

Why do I rank wasted time above wasted energy? Because I never heard anybody tell their loved ones their only regret was, "I wish I had wasted more time in my life." It's usually exactly the opposite. Wasted energy is an important issue, but rest is possible and we can come back to the issue with renewed energy. Time, however, is relentlessly constant, beating a steady cadence into eternity.

That's the issue I have with the luck strategy. To believe somehow that everything will all work out is to approach life's issues in a passive manner with no sense of urgency or purpose, which leads to no sense of direction.

Remember our model. The helicopter is your life. It carries your family, relationships, career, and health, etc., and only YOU can fly it. Others can guide you, but only you can actually move the controls and make your helicopter move in the direction you want.

This trap is akin to seeing an area in your flight route with jagged peaks, black clouds of lightning, rain, and severe turbulence and flying into it anyway. While your life is getting thrown around at the edge of controlled flight, you are saying to yourself, "This is bad, but somehow it will all work out." It doesn't make a lot of sense, but we do it all the time.

An alternative approach would be to take positive action and responsibility by seeing the dangerous conditions, proactively determining an alternative route, and executing the change. The internal dialogue would be something more like, "There's bad weather ahead. I'm going to change my route and avoid putting myself and all I care about into danger."

Another way of looking at this scenario is through Newton's First Law or the Law of Inertia, which states:

Law I: Everybody persists in its state of being at rest or of moving uniformly straight forward, except insofar as it is compelled to change its state by force impressed. (Whitman, 1999)

- An object that is at rest will stay at rest unless an unbalanced force acts upon it.

✦ An object that is in motion will not change its velocity unless an unbalanced force acts upon it.

We can usefully apply this to the dynamics of our lives, either while we're hovering or moving down the wrong path. Breaking down his law, we will see how it can apply.

The unbalanced forces mentioned above are the forces of change initiated by a personal plan. We will talk in great depth about what should go into your personal plan in part III, but I want to introduce the concept now to prep you for what's coming.

Nate: Things Will Get Back to Normal

Like most finance executives, Nate had worked hard his whole career trying to make good decisions at work and at home. He worked at his company for 14 years and had seen the company prosper as well as go through tough times.

Like many, Nate's company had been struggling for the previous few years. He had always been a pretty down-to-earth guy, living in reality and proud of his analytical abilities. Recently, however, he was starting to let himself wish for the way things used to be.

"This whole experience snuck up on me. I always thought of myself as a doer; see a problem, find its cause and fix it. I can't tell you when I changed, but somewhere along the way I started to become much less flexible. Change does take effort, and maybe I didn't want to put the effort into it anymore. Over time, I must have just become less receptive to it.

"About a year ago, I came under a lot of pressure to make my department more efficient and decided to take this time to make an investment in a new integrated enterprise system, scrapping the custom one we always used and were very comfortable with. I tell you, I just had had enough. I just became so against this project. I did everything in my power to try and stop, delay and otherwise make it fail.

"Instead of being a team player, I became somebody I never wanted to be...part of the problem."

Nate's not a bad guy; in fact he's a great guy who just happens to be human. What he didn't mention was a lot was going on in other aspects of his life during the same period. His wife, who had initially stayed home to raise their children, had become a teacher a few years earlier and was laid off because of budget cuts.

Nate also had two teenagers in the house. Although I'm sure they're great kids, teenagers are often unpredictable. Maybe Nate's resistance to change at work had something to do with trying to control at least one aspect of his life when other aspects felt so out of his control.

"The emotional response is what surprised me the most. That's not my style. I didn't have a lot of experience dealing with the way I was feeling. But after mapping out the benefits and impacts of the new system on my department, I started to realize it was a key enabler for achieving the goals the president had for me. I eventually was able to come around. I know it sounds obvious, but while it was happening all I felt was they were going to take my people away from me."

Plans and goals keep us directionally correct, even when distractions are trying to knock us off course or slow us into another hover. That's why I developed a mobile application we'll talk more about in chapter 15. But for now, it's important to understand that the benefits of having a plan are clear, especially when contrasted with the alternative.

Hover Check

✦ Has something significant changed in your life?

✦ Whatever it is, have you acknowledged that change?

✦ Do you have a plan to incorporate this change? Explain:

✦ List your action plan to incorporate the change:
  -
  -
  -
  -
  -

✦ When will your plan begin and end?

EMERGENCY PROCEDURE 9

IF YOUR LIFE HAS ENCOUNTERED SEVERE TURBULENCE AND YOU HAVE IGNORED THE INDICATIONS <u>IMMEDIATELY</u>:

- Check "Denial" is in the <u>OFF</u> position

- If change is required, <u>Acknowledge It</u>

- Then: Change your actions

IF SITUATION STILL DOES NOT IMPROVE:

- Change your situation

- Continue your mission

TM 55-1520-237-CL   E-9

CHAPTER 10

Analyzed and Paralyzed

(Ready! Aim! Aim... aim...)

Hover Trap #7

Out the right cockpit window I watched a desert weed blown by the constant whirl of my rotors. I was monitoring the radios and could hear the maneuver commanders making things happen.

"Echo 13, Echo 26, we're at phase line Saber."

"Roger 26, hold there until Charlie element catches up on your right flank, Break, Hotel 16 get your head in the game! I need smoke on Target 221."

I checked my map and tried to visualize what was happening 12 kilometers away. I shifted in my seat, checked my watch again, and scanned the instruments for the hundredth time.

"When are we going to get this show on the road?" I spoke into the intercom. Nobody in the crew responded.

This is Go Time, or, more appropriately, it *was* Go Time about ten minutes before. We had already launched two OH-58D *Kiowa Warrior*s to recon our route. They were calling back to ask where the rest of the formation was. But we were all still on the ground, loaded with troops, engines running, waiting for the launch code word.

I was the Air Mission Commander with six Blackhawks and three CH-47D Chinooks, all loaded for bear with over 200 troops, burning precious fuel and going nowhere. We waited. The word never came. Did somebody fail to make a decision? I'll never know.

Why Do Smart People Fail to Act?

In a lot of ways we, as a race, have become too smart. We have developed an environment that is increasingly complex, disruptive and unmanageable. Although I am a huge believer in the ability of individuals, teams, and organizations to overcome seemingly impossible obstacles, sometimes I can't help but wonder if we were really meant to live this way.

*Unitasking: Focusing on one task at a time.

The fact somebody found it necessary to coin the term unitasking to describe the act of, "paying attention to what you are doing," speaks volumes to the state and pace of life in the post-information age. They talk about unitasking as if focus, concentration and stick-to-itiveness were new concepts.

Today, we have plenty of data and knowledge at our fingertips to apply to any situation we encounter. There are so many alternatives and consequences to our actions or inactions we can easily fall into the "Analyzed and Paralyzed" hover trap.

As we explore this trap, we will look at the cost of doing nothing or not moving forward with the things that should mean the most to us: our families, relationships, careers, and health.

I say, *"Doing nothing,"* but to be more precise, I mean, *"Doing nothing after identifying the issues, possible courses of action, possible consequences of courses of action, and cost in time and energy to accomplish any particular course of action."* If this sounds like you, keep reading.

Ann Langley, professor of Administrative Science at the University of Quebec, Montreal, identifies and studies the continuum between Paralysis by Analysis and Extinction by Instinct. (Langley, 1995) Fundamentally, she found the overriding need for extreme analysis has a lot to do with personality type,

> *"...for example, individual aptitudes and preferences for analytical or intuitive thinking. In this case, paralysis by analysis would be associated with people who are naturally drawn to numbers, while the reverse (extinction by instinct) would be associated with impulsive managers with intuitive cognitive styles."*

This begs the question, what kind of thinker are you? Are you prone to overanalyze? Are you impulsive? More importantly, is the level of analysis dependent on the topic or situation? The answer should jump right out at you. If it doesn't, don't stop thinking about it. Look back to important decisions you made in your life and determine where you land on the continuum.

A useful way to visualize these tendencies is with the Quadrants of Action and Analysis Chart shown in figure 11-1. Everybody has certain built-in tendencies. It is always useful to understand your own so you can make better decisions from a place of clarity.

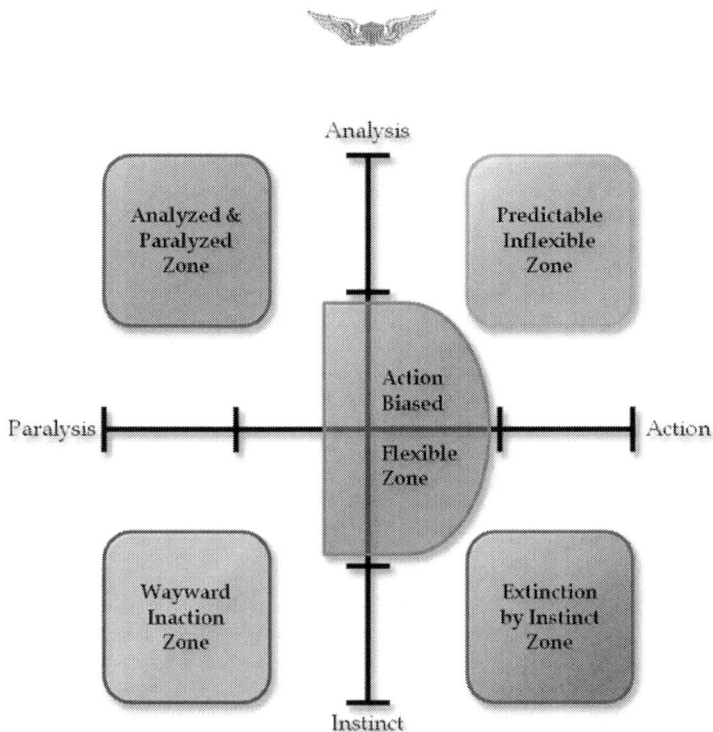

Figure 11-1: The Quadrants of Action and Analysis chart illustrates individual and organizational decision-making agility

Analyzed & Paralyzed Zone: As much of this chapter discusses, this quadrant is a place where too much analysis impedes action. Action is required to effect change. This zone stops individuals and organizations from getting out of the hover. Use analysis to confirm or deny your instincts or vice versa.

Predictable Inflexible Zone: Extreme analysis and action may seem like an obvious double positive and it can be. Fact-driven scenarios combined with action can move any issue forward. The only caution is that this zone may be too inflexible, not allowing for adaptation and course corrections. Be aware of it.

Wayward Inaction Zone: What can I say? This is a double negative. Not only is there an inability to act, there is also no analysis. A structured plan coupled with tools to understand how to organize issues and set priorities will help in this zone. Success in the quadrant is a low probability happenstance that will be short-lived.

Extinction by Instinct Zone: Action all the time but guided by the gut. When an individual or organization operates from pure emotion, actions are often erratic and susceptible to blind spots. These blind spots will lead to large, unforeseen setbacks. More analysis must be injected into the decision process in this quadrant.

Action Biased Flexible Zone: Obviously with the balanced approach you will notice a distinct favoring of action but with a healthy mix of both instinct AND analysis. Look at the area slightly left of the vertical axis. It's there because sometimes the right move is to wait to see how things develop. Action for action's sake is not the goal. Understanding why we're acting is fundamental.

The situational component cannot be overlooked. For example, you might know every technical specification regarding an automobile purchase but navigate career decisions based on feel and fit issues. Is there too much or too little analysis? It doesn't matter. Was there enough analysis for you to make a timely decision? That's what matters.

Important decisions warrant an appropriate amount of thoughtful research. What you must weigh is if the amount of research, modeling, and simulations of outcomes relating to a directionally correct, timely decision is worth the risk of waiting.

In a sense, I'm asking, "What's the opportunity cost of the delay?"

Rajesh Setty, business author, speaker, and consultant, in his article, "Why Some Smart People Don't Take Action," explains a compelling theory for why successful professionals get stuck in the analysis hover. (Setty, 2010) To Setty, it is a question of Current Capacity vs. Threshold of Capacity.

Do you have the need to continually put off any decision because you are never quite "ready?"

He asserts smart people know enough to evaluate the state of their current capabilities and how to estimate what their capabilities need to be to assure success in their future plans, career, interpersonal, physical, or otherwise. The gap analysis calculus is the easy part, initially. But what often happens is what Langley calls "The Vicious Circle," where analysis instead of accomplishment is the ammunition in a battle. (Langley 1995)

What does this mean? Remember my initial assertion: We have become too smart. If you are prone to analysis and smart enough to conduct a gap analysis, you are also smart enough to take the initial actions to close the gap in capabilities or experience.

This is depicted in Figure 11-2.

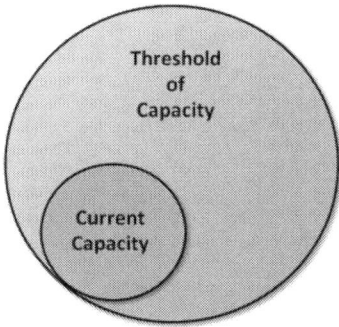

Figure 11-2 Today(T)   Figure 11-3 T+2

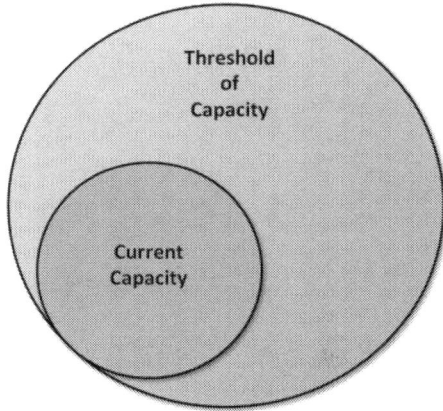

To grow our capabilities we might enroll in a MBA program, seek new challenges at work, or join a gym and get fit. It all depends in what aspect of your life you are looking to close the gap.

Invariably, what we learn shows us we need to know more than we previously expected. Naturally, current capacity has grown but the threshold of capacity has grown, too. Notice the relative size of both the current capacity and threshold of capacity in Figure 11-3.

This cycle can continue indefinitely. Grow current capacity only to learn more, understand more, and fuel the need to continually put off any decision because we are never quite ready.

Have you ever found yourself putting off decisions or actions because the time is just not right? There's a good chance you are in this hover trap. You're expending precious energy and resources only to go nowhere. The cost in time wasted can be considerable.

Fear

We have to talk about it. Most of us don't want to admit that fear is the reason behind our excuses and rationalizations about why we can't move forward. I used to think fear was not an obstacle for smart, accomplished people. I was wrong.

What I have found is even successful people feel fear. For some it's the reason they are successful. For others it's the reason they are not.

> *"Many high performers would rather do the wrong thing well than do the right thing poorly."*
>
> *- Thomas & Sara DeLong*

In a recent Harvard Business Review article, both Thomas DeLong and Sara DeLong uncovered some common blind spots high-achieving professionals possess. Read the following examples they came up with and see if you can spot yourself in some of them. I could.

- **Driven to get results:** Achievers don't let anything stop them. However, they can get so caught up in a task that providing transparency to colleagues or helping others feels like a waste of valuable time.
- **A Doer:** Achievers believe, often rightly, that nobody can do it as well as they can. That can make them poor delegators or micromanagers.
- **Highly motivated:** Achievers take all aspects of their jobs seriously. But that means they often fail to distinguish between the urgent and the merely important.

- **Craving positive feedback:** Achievers care intensely about how others view their work but they tend to ignore positive feedback and obsess over criticism.
- **Competitive:** An appetite for competition is healthy but achievers obsessively compare themselves with others, which can lead to a chronic sense of insufficiency, false calibrations, and ultimately career missteps.
- **Passionate about work:** Intense highs can give way to crippling lows. For achievers, it's a fine line between triumph and agony.
- **A safe risk taker:** Achievers aren't likely to recklessly bet the company on a risky move but they may shy away from the unknown.
- **Guilt-ridden:** Achievers are driven to produce but no matter how much they accomplish, they feel like they aren't doing enough. (DeLong, 2011)

If these characteristics describe you, then you might be susceptible to this trap. I want you to make a commitment right now to:

- Identify your fear(s)
- Evaluate your fear(s)
- Create a goal (who, what, when, where) to achieve or overcome your fear(s)
- Develop action steps to support the goal (how)
- Understand you will have to adjust the plan (adapt)
- Remain oriented on your goal (focus)

The Good News about a Hover

Yes, there is good news. Back to our metaphor. If we are hovering, that implies we are, in fact, already flying. We already know we possess the capacity to lift ourselves. We have control of ourselves and now just need to harness the power we are already demonstrating in a more useful way.

Take some time to jot down answers to the above steps.

If you're reading this book, I'm assuming you have a highly developed skill-set and the intellect to use it.

But, to be frank, it's easy to assess a situation, conduct a course of action analysis, and make a plan. It is difficult to accomplish the above *AND* then gather the resources, create the buy-in, and execute the plan.

Hover Check

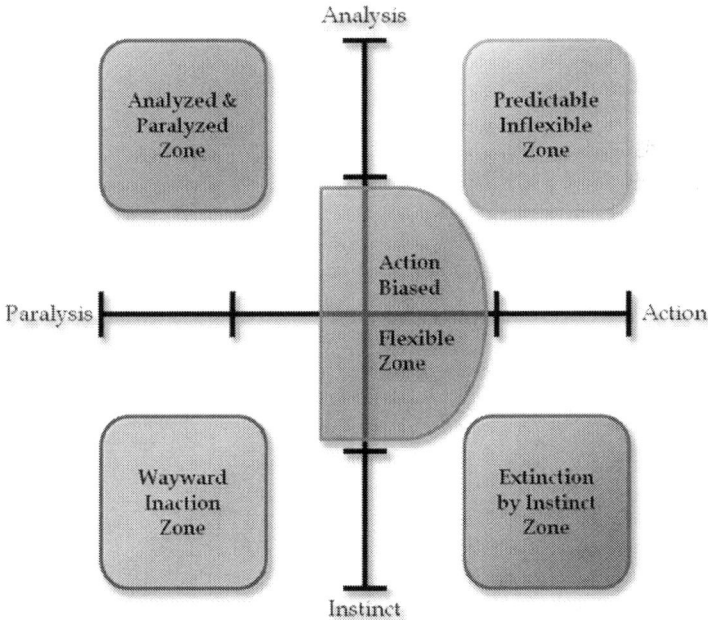

Review this diagram. In which zone do you most find yourself?

List the steps you are going to take to move yourself into the Action Biased, Flexible Zone:

1.
2.
3.
4.
5.

EMERGENCY PROCEDURE 10

IF PARALYSIS BY ANALYSIS OR EXTINCTION BY INSTINCT <u>OCCURS</u>:

- Identify the issue

- Evaluate the issue

- Create a goal (who, what, when, where)

- Develop action steps that support achieving or overcoming the issue (how)

- Be open to adjusting the plan (adapt)

- Stay oriented on the goal (focus)

<u>PERFECTION IS NOT REQUIRED - PROGRESS IS</u>

TM 55-1520-237-CL   E-10

CHAPTER 11

Focus on Everything
(and Get Nothing Done)
Hover Trap #8

I could smell the cordite from artillery shells that had just exploded. Quickly checking the map, GPS, and clock, we were on our route and on time. Ahead in the distance my goggles picked up flashes from more exploding artillery rounds. Behind me, the crew chief had 200 live rounds loaded in his door gun. Behind him were 14 heavily armed infantrymen, faces blacked out.

Deliberately weaving through the terrain, the six aircraft behind me carried identical loads. We were going to drop these men at the doorstep of an enemy-held hill complex. They would be delivered in the dead of night, undaunted by the darkness.

Modern combined arms doctrine is a highly refined extension of Blitzkrieg warfare. Using all the assets available to the commander, in this case artillery, Cobra gunships, UH-60s, and infantry, we would overwhelm and destroy the enemy before they had a chance to defend themselves. Modern warfare is not a fair fight.

This night, the 105 Howitzers covered the gunships' and troop-carrying helicopters' approach by targeting known and suspected positions along our routes. This keeps the enemy looking for cover instead of looking for us. Once the gunships get into position, they suppress the objective with their 20mm cannons as the artillery shifts to the objective and other avenues of approach that could bring reinforcements.

Rounding a small hill, I see the tracers from the gunship's cannon. We're still on time and on target. As we approach our Landing Zone (LZ), the door gunners start firing. The aircraft shakes from the recoil. They are suppressing the immediate area as the gunships shift their fire away from us. Finally, we land. Soldiers jump out and take the hill while we disappear into the night.

During the mission, I monitored four radios, made position reports, navigated, and ensured we were making our time windows. (The other pilot was flying.) Timing is the key to safety and keeping pressure on the enemy.

Photo 11-1 Delivering combat power to the battle is what air assault is all about. (Courtesy US Army)

During the final and most important phase of delivering the men, I focused only on the few most important tasks. I stowed the map, let the radio chatter fall away, and positioned my hands a hovering inch from the controls, just in case.

The mission I just described was part of a larger training exercise and was observed by dignitaries and heads of foreign air arms. The ammunition was real, the night was real, the helicopters were real, and the danger was real. I multitasked during non-critical periods of the mission and focused intensely during the most important and dangerous times.

There is a lesson you will learn from this story as you read on. Needless to say, multitasking often makes sense, but there are times when it doesn't. Having the ability to discern when and when not to multitask is essential to long-term success in our relationships, career, and getting the most out of ourselves.

Do you understand Focus?

- *Close one eye and focus on any one object in front of you.*
- *Now try to focus on only two objects at the same time. Three? Four?*
- *Our eye is telling us something profound.*
- *By definition, focus means affixing our attention on a singular and finite area.*

Figure 11-1 In today's world, focus is becoming a lost art.

Multitasking, a skill needed to fly a helicopter, has become a way of life for most of us. It makes sense. If we are faced with ever increasing tasks, we respond by increasing our rate of work and finally splitting our attention between multiple tasks. This works…for a while.

The "I'll Focus on Everything" trap is a natural destination for many of us, but if we stay in the place where everything is important, we are really saying nothing is important.

Although we cannot completely do away with multitasking, I want to make the point clearly that there are limits to its benefits. Work in the study of multitasking will shed light on and guide us toward strategies we can employ to get the most from our time and effort.

- *High Multitasker: Those who routinely used four, five or more media at one time. (texting, reading email, talking on the phone, watching video, etc.)*
- *Low Multitasker: Those who routinely used, on average, no more than two media at one time.*

A recent study by Stanford University, published in "Proceedings of the National Academy of Sciences" (Clifford Nass, 2009), uncovered three fundamental issues with multitasking and the "I'll Focus on Everything" trap.

The research was set up like this: 100 volunteers, both self-described high multitaskers and low multitaskers, participated. The study focused on what elements of multitasking the high multitaskers excelled at compared to the low multitaskers. Nass defined three core traits required for effective multitasking. The three aspects the study examined were:

  ✦ Filtering Environmental Distractions: The ability to focus on the relevant and ignore the irrelevant. To multitask well, one must be able to quickly triage what is important, what to pay attention to, and what is irrelevant.

☀ Filtering Irrelevant Representations in Memory: The ability to keep information well organized in the brain. Nass likes to use the analogy of the brain as a collection of filing cabinets. The more organized files equal more efficient and faster information retrieval.

☀ Task Switching: Being able to switch from one task to another. The ability to mentally go from one activity to the next, without significant cognitive downtime, is also required to be a good multitasker.

The results surprised the researchers as well as me. The high multitaskers did worse in all three aspects than the low multitaskers.

Let's look at the first aspect: Filtering Environmental Distractions, the ability to focus on the relevant and ignore the irrelevant. The high multitaskers showed a shocking lack of ability to discern relevant from irrelevant information. Nass stated, "High multitaskers are suckers for irrelevancy. Everything distracts them."

> *The high multitaskers showed a shocking lack of ability to discern relevant from irrelevant information.*

In fact, not everybody is a fan of multitasking. Dr. Edward Hallowell, a Massachusetts-based psychiatrist specializing in attention deficit/hyperactivity disorder and author of a book entitled *CrazyBusy*, states multi-tasking is "mythical activity in which people believe they can perform two or more tasks simultaneously." (Rosen, 2008) Timothy Ferriss, in his book, *The 4-Hour Workweek,* emphasizes the power of single-tasking to be more productive and effective. (Ferriss 2007)

Photo 11-2 Like your life without priorities, the cockpit of a helicopter while flying formation, navigating, and monitoring multiple radios, can quickly become a hectic, confusing and unhealthy place. Photo by (Travis Zielinski)

Now let's look at the second aspect: Filtering Irrelevant Representations in Memory, the ability to keep information well organized in the brain. The high multitaskers had messier file cabinets than their counterparts and had difficulty retrieving information on request.

Russell Poldrack thinks he knows why. A psychology professor at the University of Texas at Austin, Poldrack has studied the human brain using MRI technology. He has determined that when a person is learning a new task while distracted or multitasking, the active part of the brain is the striatum, which is associated with rewards and novelty.

Alternatively, people who learned while focused activated the hippocampus, a different region of the brain associated with storing and recalling information. (Poldrack, 2006)

Lastly, let's consider the third aspect: Task Switching, being able to switch from one task to another in the shortest amount of time. The more the high multitaskers were required to switch their task, the worse they were at it. Meaning it took them longer to get up to speed on the task to which they'd just switched. Think of this as that uncomfortable pause or blankness in our minds after being asked a question and waiting for our brains to find the answer.

Rene Marois, in a recent study, explains a "Control Bottleneck" of information processing. (Marois, 2005) If the brain is forced to respond to several things at once, time is lost processing a response.

A study from the University of California at Irvine concluded it took on average 25 minutes for office workers to recover from common interruptions like a phone call or responding to an email. (Rosen, 2008) In the semiconductor industry, it's referred to as propagation delay, the amount of time from input to output. In the aviation world, we used to call it a helmet fire. Either way, changing from task to task takes time and energy.

The irony is this: Almost to a person, the self-proclaimed high multitaskers insisted they were very good at it! All in all, severe multitasking is a direct detriment to our personal and organizational productivity. If time is money, multitasking is wasting a whole lot of both.

Wayne: I'm Working on It

Busy but not effective just doesn't cut it. Everybody is busy, but it takes discipline to be more effective. I know firsthand because, if there is one trap I find myself in most, it's this one. So when Wayne contacted me, I had an extra dose of empathy for him. Can you see a little of yourself in his story?

"I'm in technology and things are always evolving. To keep up with it all, I thought I needed to subscribe to every technology group, blog and newsletter. When one of them popped up on my computer, I had to read it right then. I regularly stayed late or brought work home to finish. I tried making to-do lists but still found myself falling behind. I started to feel like I was a slave to my work."

"I admit I liked doing things I enjoyed and would quickly set aside tasks I didn't for another time. By practicing what Ken calls Punctuated Focus, I've been able to build a discipline of focusing longer on items that need to get done. It's increased my productivity and taken some of the stress off me because I don't have to bring as much work home and everybody is happy about that."

"At first it was very hard to not reach for my phone or click on my emails, but I got better at only checking those things once an hour. I still work at it every day."

What stands out to me about what Wayne said is that the transformation from multitasker to a more focused unitasker is a process that takes time and energy. A habit is hard to break, especially if you've had it for a long time. But, like everything, we can break out of this hover, too.

What to Do about It

If this is your trap, try some of these techniques to move yourself from multitasker to unitasker. I call it Punctuated Focus because, in many ways, it mirrors Dr. Gould's theory. It calls for us to focus on a single task, to get deep into it, understand it, and get it done. This activates the hippocampus, or file cabinet, of your brain and stores it away for use at another time.

Focus does take energy but like a muscle the more you work it the stronger it gets. Even so, we need a break and that's the punctuated side of this equation. Every 50 minutes, take a breather and come up for air. Return calls and emails during this time. You are resting your brain between sets in a workout.

All of the following techniques require only one thing: You becoming the Pilot in Command of your life. Try them and see if you get more done, faster and better.

- Designate task times: Plan your day the evening before. Cluster like tasks together as much as possible. For example, make calls from 9:00 – 9:45, finish a report from 10:00 – 10:45. Make a plan and stick to it. It's time for you to attack the day, not for the day to assault you.
- Capture all new to-dos the same way, every time, and write them down. When we're under pressure, we subconsciously switch into emergency action mode and blindly react. Instead write them down, avoiding the temptation to do them immediately and throwing your plan to the wind.
- Unitask with technology. Because information can changed so quickly, we have been conditioned to want to

respond immediately. Check emails, voicemails, texts, holograms from outer space, once an hour.

✦ De-clutter your desk. (This even applies to those who claim they can find anything in that big stack of papers.) If we are trying to de-clutter our brains, why not the desk to match?

✦ Clear your computer desktop. Put everything in virtual folders and label them properly.

✦ Don't needlessly open multiple programs on your computer. Open one, complete the task, then close before you go on to the next step and the next program to complete your day's work. Be organized and your work will be too.

✦ Don't constantly chit-chat with colleagues. It's good to be friendly, but it's better to get your work done. Sometimes this can only be accomplished by telling others in advance that you're on a deadline.

✦ It's a good idea not to maniacally IM and Tweet. Also, try turning your new email notification off. Check e-mails periodically, close the program, and move on.

Try some of these techniques and you're on your way to transforming busy into effective. Also, you may find you have time to chit-chat with colleagues, maniacally IM, play Angry Birds or Tweet on your own terms (just kidding). An entire book can be written just about dealing with email effectively, and in fact, I know the authors of the best one, *Slay the E-mail Monster.* (Coffman, 2010) Lynn Coffman and Michael Valentine are productivity experts and their book is worth its weight in gold.

Hover Check

✦ Do you still consider yourself a proficient multitasker?

✦ Try the concept of Punctuated Focus for one week. What aspect of your life will you use it in: family, friends, career/business, health, or spiritual life?

✦ Have you discovered a habit or habits making you less productive than you easily could be? Take the time now to list them here:

EMERGENCY PROCEDURE 11

IF YOU THINK YOU ARE A GOOD MULTITASKER IMMEDIATELY KNOW YOU ARE NOT:

— Are you easily distracted?

— Having trouble recalling recent information?

— Spending a lot of time getting "Back Up to Speed" after switching tasks?

CHECK:

— Unitasking Switch is in the ON POSTION

— Focus on your task until completion

TM 55-1520-237-CL   E-11

126

Target Fixation
Hover Trap #9

Now, you may be saying to yourself, "Hold it, Ken. In the last chapter you said we shouldn't try to focus on everything at once and now you're saying don't focus on just one thing. You can't have it both ways."

You're right. I can't have it both ways. But, like I mentioned in the introduction to Part II, these traps are not absolute. We can fall into multiple traps to differing degrees and not fall into others altogether.

For example, the person who possesses a propensity to focus on only one thing is not the same person who tries to focus on everything. If it helps you, think of chapter 11 and chapter 12 as different sides of the same coin.

The Cost of Target Fixation

While researching this topic, I asked a lot of current attack helicopter pilots if they ever experienced target fixation. Many had but none of them wanted me to write about their experiences. I don't blame them. Instead, I went back in history and didn't have to look far to find examples of this trap.

Photo 12-1 AH-1G Cobra inverted. (Courtesy VHPA)

Read the abridged crash reports from Vietnam identifying individuals who were killed by this trap. I found the matter-of-fact, succinct descriptions chilling.

- Jan 1969: Pleiku Province: Exploded in the air after hitting trees on a low-level gun run.
- Aug 1969: Quang Nam Province: Aircraft was making gun runs on the target. The aircraft was observed to pull out late and "mush" into the ground in a near level attitude.
- Sept 1969: Binh Duong Province: Aircraft flew into the ground on a gun run.
- Jan 1970: An Xugen Province: Flew into the ground on a gun run at night.
- July 1970: Thua Thien Province: Crashed during night possibly due to vertigo or target fixation.
- Aug 1970: Binh Duong Province: Flew into target on Nighthawk fire mission outside Phouc Vinh perimeter.
- Mar 1971: Vinh Bonh Province: Aircraft failed to pull out of a night gun run.
- May 1971: Quang Tri Province: Aircraft crashed possibly due to hostile fire or pulling out of a gun run too low to clear the trees.
- Sept 1971: Long An Province: Aircraft crashed and exploded in a bunker south of fire support base Mace, probably from target fixation. (Allen)

Target fixation is real and can be a killer in your life, flying or not. Is it possible to be too focused? To be so intent on one thing that all other things, even incredibly important things, drop away from your view? Read on and see if this information applies to you or somebody you know.

Loss of Perspective

You might be asking yourself, "How hard can it be to not hit the ground?" Federal Aviation Administration statistics show between 5 to 10% of all general aviation accidents can be attributed to spatial disorientation, 90% of which are fatal. (Melchor Antunano, 2010)

We must understand two definitions. The first is Spatial Disorientation, and the second is called Target Fixation or Target Hypnosis. Both these definitions describe a physiological loss of perspective.

Spatial Disorientation: *An individual's inability to determine his or her position, attitude, and motion relative to the surface of the earth or significant objects; for example, trees, poles, or buildings during hover. When it occurs, pilots are unable to see, believe, interpret, or prove the information derived from their flight instruments. Instead, they rely on the false information that their senses provide.* (FM 1-301 Aeromedical Training for Flight Personnel, Dept of Army, 1987) For our purposes, the "false" information could be from emotional reactions or skewed past experiences rather than from facts.

Target Fixation: *Occurs when an aircrew member ignores orientation cues and focuses his attention on his object or goal; for example, an attack pilot on a gunnery range becomes so intent on hitting the target that he forgets to fly the aircraft, resulting in it striking the ground, the target, or the shrapnel created by hitting the* *target.* (FM 1-301 Aeromedical Training for Flight Personnel, Dept of Army, 1987)

Target fixation differs from spatial disorientation because the intensity of our focus is so great we let other important cues drop from our attention.

Photo 12-2 Staying aware of your surroundings will give you clues when it's time to pull up and away from your target in both an attack helicopter and life. (Courtesy US Army)

For a Kamikaze, target fixation is probably a good thing, but for the rest of us it is definitely not. Unfortunately, it takes multiple cues to keep us oriented. When target fixation occurs while flying or in our lives,

How do we know we have target fixation in an aspect of our lives?

it means we have lost our perspective and are ignoring important cues. Making good decisions is almost impossible.

Enter the Truth Room and ask yourself these questions: Can you think of a time in your life when you locked on to just one thing and lost your perspective of the things that kept you oriented? Are you in this trap now?

How do we know we have target fixation? It's when your thoughts and actions are focused almost solely on only one aspect of your life. Taken to its extreme, target fixation could turn into unhealthy obsessive behavior.

Most of us never let it get that far. To determine if you are in this trap, examine the other important aspects of your life to see if they are being neglected. Is your family suffering, your relationships, career, health, your spiritual life?

Maintaining Perspective

Just like trying to focus on everything gets us nowhere, focusing only on one thing will rapidly degrade into disorientation, bad decisions, and harm to us and the ones we care about.

One time, my copilot suffered the effects of vertigo while flying an instrument approach in the clouds. Suddenly he said, "You have the controls!" I grabbed them quickly and continued the approach. From the corner of my eye I could see his body slumped against the door. He was definitely disoriented; not knowing which way was up.

It was essential to have a system to keep us from becoming disoriented. Pilots call it the instrument crosscheck, also known as the scan. The only way spatial disorientation can creep into a pilot's head is if they slow or stop their scan of the instruments.

When I was flying, I always did my scan the same way every time. I always started with airspeed and went clockwise from there. It went something like this:

1. Airspeed: Set and constant
2. Artificial Horizon: Attitude correct, wings level
3. Altitude Indicator: Climb/Descent correct
4. Vertical Situation Indicator: Rate of Climb/Descent set and constant
5. Horizontal Situation Indicator: Course correct and constant
6. Power: Check

See Figure 12-1 to see what the cockpit instruments of a Blackhawk look like.

The noise, vibration, and variations of light coming into the cockpit are constant threats to your situational awareness. If I started to feel the creep of disorientation, I increased the speed of my scan, increasing the data reference points to my brain.

Why?

Every instrument is telling me what my orientation is to the surface of the earth. Those six indicators combined gave me a mental picture of what my aircraft was doing in time and space. This firm picture of reality, constantly being updated by another iteration of a scan, kept me out of trouble.

Your Personal Cockpit

What if we could take this concept and apply it to our lives? If we could create a personal cockpit, complete with indicators feeding us information about the condition of our life, would it help us stay on track, in balance, out of hovers and target fixation?

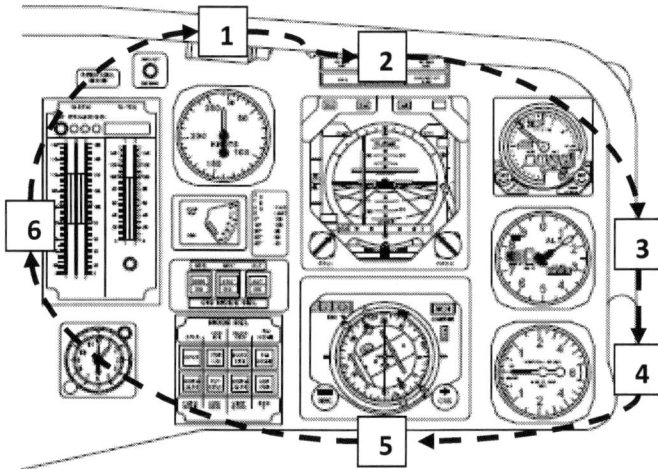

Figure12-1 Cockpit Instrument Scan

By developing your personal instruments and indicators, you too can have a firm picture of the reality around you. The chances are you already have most of them. But, look for the blind spots, the aspects of your life where surprises and trouble have occurred in the past.

Is it a relationship indicator, health indicator, balance indicator, or career speed indicator? Only you can decide but, like the instruments in a cockpit tell the pilot what's really happening, your indicators must tell you the same. A good starting point might be the five life aspects we've mentioned already: family, friends, career/business, health, and spiritual life.

Target Fixated Tom

What do you do when a person's greatest characteristic in business is also their greatest obstacle to happiness? At first, I didn't know either. When I met Tom I was immediately impressed. He had energy, a ton of it, but when he would pause and think I could detect something else. At first I didn't know what it was. I can only think of one word when I think back to those times: Strain.

"I have always been a very detail oriented person. It's probably why I got my engineering degree. When I was promoted to Director of Engineering of a high-tech firm, things seemed to just go out of control. There was never enough time and the pace I had to deal with was overwhelming.

"I realized my natural tendency to drill down and focus on one task at a time, which served me so well as an engineer, was actually leading me to failure as a manager. It was quickly becoming a disaster as I focused on one task until completion and missed other important deadlines."

In the end I think we both figured it out together.

Everybody is different but in your life you have knowingly or unknowingly developed your own way to stay oriented. Like my crosscheck, each of these data points will give you a little bit of information to collectively create a clear picture of your situation and not allow you to lose perspective.

If you don't have a system, can you see how you might make the same missteps again and again? Making a mistake is simply being human, continuing to repeatedly make the same mistakes borders on buffoonery. Nobody has time for that.

Hover Check

🪶 Can you think of a time in your life when you locked on to just one thing and lost your perspective on the other things that kept you oriented?

🪶 Are you experiencing target fixation in your life right now? What is it?

🪶 Remember your scan. List the instruments that will keep you oriented:

EMERGENCY PROCEDURE 12

IF ONE ASPECT OF YOUR LIFE IS REQUIRING YOU TO NEGLECT THE OTHERS YOU HAVE ENTERED:

+ Target Fixation

IMMEDIATELY:

+ Initiate your SCAN

+ Assess other aspects of your life

+ Make corrective actions

+ Continue to monitor your situation

+ Continue your mission

TM 55-1520-237-CL   E-12

CHAPTER 13

It's All My Fault

Hover Trap #10

Under grey skies and above rough seas the first of 16 B-25B Mitchell bombers lifted off the timber deck of the USS Hornet. It was April 18, 1942, a little over five months after the Japanese attack on Pearl Harbor. At the controls was the mission leader, the then Lieutenant Colonel (LTC) James "Jimmy" Doolittle.

The now-famous Doolittle Raid was never meant to be a one-way trip. The original plan was to get the USS Hornet 450 miles from Japan and launch the aircraft, fly low to avoid radar, attack industrial targets, and continue to China.

Photo 13-1 In rough seas, Doolittle's B-25 lifts off the deck of the USS Hornet. Like all good leaders, Doolittle led from the front. His was the first aircraft to launch that day. (Courtesy US Naval Historical Center)

In China, an electronic beacon was to be set up at an airfield to guide the bombers to safety. Once landed, they would be refueled and flown farther west to India. At least, that was the plan.

When a picket ship was spotted approximately 200 miles from their intended take-off point, the decision was made to launch regardless, knowing there might not be enough fuel to make it to China.

Doolittle and his raiders would consider themselves lucky to survive the day.

Also, Doolittle didn't know the beacons never made it to their intended destination. There would be no way for the bombers to find their landing strip. Even though he didn't know it at the time, Doolittle and his raiders would consider themselves lucky to survive the day. (Glines, 1989)

After bombing their assigned targets, all 16 aircraft continued to China observing radio silence. With no beacon, fading light, and fuel almost exhausted, the pilot in command of every bomber had to make an unenviable decision to either ditch or bail out of their aircraft.

The next morning, Doolittle found the wreckage of his aircraft. He realized all of the airplanes under his command must have met the same fate. He feared the worst and with good reason. In the end, all his planes were indeed lost, eight crew members were captured, and eventually five crew members died either by execution or drowning. One died because his parachute failed to open.

Photo 13-2 A dejected Doolittle ponders his situation amongst the wreckage of his aircraft in China. (Courtesy US Naval Historical Center)

As Jimmy Doolittle sat, dejected, he mentioned to one of his crew he thought he would most likely be court-martialed and sent to jail when he returned to the United States.

> *He thought he would be court-martialed and sent to jail.*

Looking at it from his perspective, I can see why he felt that way. Doolittle quite justifiably could have hung his head in defeat and given up, but he didn't. Instead, with the help of many Chinese, he energetically started coordinating the gathering and movement of all the crew members. Doolittle didn't let himself get caught feeling sorry for himself. He continued to be an effective leader.

When Doolittle returned to the United States, he was not court-martialed or thrown in jail. He and his raiders returned to the United States as national heroes. Doolittle was promoted from LTC directly to Brigadier General, skipping Colonel!

Photo 13-3 Portrait of Doolittle, 1942. (Courtesy US Naval Historical Center)

He flew over the beaches of Normandy on D-Day and commanded the mighty 8th Air Force in Europe. His career wasn't over. The greatest part of it was just beginning. General Doolittle did not let his perceived setback define him. When put in perspective, his mission was not a failure but a great success and we can all take something away from his story.

When Things Go Wrong

I can't tell you why bad things happen to us but in this life we are constantly challenged with obstacles that we must negotiate and overcome. For the most part, we have no control over what happens to us but we do possess all the control when it comes to how we react to real setbacks in our lives.

Before we can move to the "how" of setbacks and loss, we must first take a little time to understand the "what" of them. Ask yourself these questions to help determine the facts:

- What happened?
- Is the situation a significant loss or just a frustrating setback?
- In what aspect of your life did this event occur:
- Family
- Friend
- Career/Business
- Health
- Spiritual Life?
- What other aspects does this event affect?
- List some realistic actions you can take now.

Take the time to write down a short narrative of the events and most importantly how you feel about them. If you do this exercise in the Truth Room, good information should come out of it. The more complex and personal the event, the more important it is to go through this exercise. Use the space at the end of this chapter to write your answers. Go there now and fill it out. It will help.

Dealing with the Blame Game

When things go wrong it is too easy to look for someone or something to blame. Resist this temptation with all your might and instead focus your energy on trying to understand what has happened. This isn't easy and admittedly goes against our darker but normal human nature. However, by focusing on the facts of a situation, we can possibly turn a very bad situation into a much more positive one for us and others.

By no means am I suggesting criminals should go unpunished, that justice should not be brought to bear. Of course this should happen. However, I'm most interested in how we let the need for affixing blame, seeking revenge, and exacting retribution take all our energy and focus away from moving toward our important goals.

A great difference exists between a significant loss and a frustrating setback or obstacle. Some losses are more significant than others but all losses and setbacks need to be dealt with, resolved (at least understood), mined for meaningful lessons, and filed away, especially if they are stopping you from having the life you want for yourself.

"I have the controls."

For many of us an event happened, maybe even decades ago, that has derailed a certain aspect of our life. The pain was so great we are afraid of even thinking about addressing it. So what do we do?

Nothing. We don't deal with it. We try to move on with our lives. The problem is no matter where we go or how far we travel, it will always be tagging along until we deal with it. We may have been wronged, hurt, swindled, abused, or lied to. Regardless of what happened, we gave a negative event more control over us than it ever should have.

We may have relinquished the controls of our helicopter to this event without even realizing it. If that's the case with you, say out loud, "I have the controls." That's exactly what a pilot says when they take over the controls of an aircraft from another pilot. Say it and do it, "I have the controls."

Andrew: I Won't Go There Again

An accomplished marketing executive, Andrew's career was on the rise. He had accepted his dream job to manage all the marketing of a large sporting venue in a large metropolitan area. He was on top of the world and looking forward to making an impact. Unfortunately, what should have been a highlight of his career quickly turned into a long-lasting painful memory.

"It's really true. People don't leave jobs, they leave managers. When the economy turned down we were affected, too. The campaigns I was running started to perform below expectation. It was to be expected. The whole economy was sliding. I didn't like it, but I could understand it. The general manager had other ideas of why business was down: Me.

"What started as increased involvement in the strategy and planning eventually escalated into brutal, vicious verbal abuse. It was more devastating than I imagined. My first reaction was he must be having a very bad day but the bad day turned into weeks and then months. I tried everything I could to please him, but at the time, macroeconomics were also at play.

"I worked so hard to get to where I was in my career. I finally got to the point where I told myself I wasn't going to let this miserable person run me out. I decided to dig in and hold on tight, but when the end game finally played out, I was asked to leave.

"I hadn't realized how traumatized I was. I had gained weight, developed a tick in my right eye, and felt my professional and personal confidence had been torn from my body. For the life of me I couldn't get myself to even look for another position. I just couldn't bring myself to engage mentally. I didn't even look for a job for about four months. Like I said, he really did a number on me. I'll never let that happen to me again."

It took some time for Andrew to truly believe that given a different boss and environment he would have been wildly successful without changing any of his actions. Over time, Andrew has put this experience in a place where he could once again move forward in his personal and professional life. Andrew is back on his game after his experience. Are you? If not, keep reading.

> **"Don't get mad, don't get even; get ahead."**
> *- Chris Matthews*

Chris Matthews, in his book *Hardball,* wrote a chapter entitled, "Don't Get Mad; Don't Get Even; Get Ahead." (Matthews, 1999) As the title suggests, regardless of whether somebody wronged you or something bad happened to you, the most productive thing for you to do is stay focused on your goals. These are good words to live by. Why would we let one bad event have that kind of control over us? Don't waste the time. You have a mission to complete.

Accept the Healing Where and When It Comes

In 1969, psychiatrist Elisabeth Kubler-Ross wrote one of the most influential books about dying. *On Death and Dying* introduces the concept of the five stages of loss: Denial, Anger, Bargaining, Depression, and Acceptance, commonly referred to as DABDA. (Kubler-Ross, 1969)

Russell Friedman, the Executive Director of the Grief Recovery Institute and co-author of *The Grief Recovery Handbook* and *When Children Grieve,* thinks we should rethink DABDA, and so do I. During the 1970s, the topic of Kubler-Ross' widely accepted book was also applied to the concepts of grief and loss, never its intended purpose. (Friedman, 2008)

The stages of dying or loss are now very familiar and have been applied to change management, divorce, job loss, and other situations. It's a useful model. It's clean, easy and, in its current understanding, completely flawed. Let me explain.

Implying there is a rigid process we all go through is not only wrong but possibly harmful.

When we are faced with a major loss or setback, we all want to understand what is going on emotionally within us. Our society has come to expect definitive answers immediately and I mean *right now*. We want to be able to put "A" into the DABDA model and know in six months "B" will come out. It just doesn't work that way. (Friedman, 2008)

Friedman argues that implying there is a rigid process we all go through is not only wrong but possibly harmful. We process information differently. We react to loss differently.

Some will accept a loss immediately and never feel the other stages. Others may get stuck in the anger stage and never get to acceptance. DABDA is a tool to be used like any other tool. Use it to understand what you're feeling if it helps you. Don't automatically expect you will go through all five stages in a rigid order or time period. It's important to look for understanding and healing. Accept them where and when they come.

Hover Check

✦ Have you had a setback you just can't shake? Privately write it down here:

✦ What lessons did you learn from it? Privately list them here:

✦ Who has the controls?

EMERGENCY PROCEDURE 13

IF A SIGNIFICANT EVENT, HANG-UP, OR
HOVER TRAP <u>EXISTS</u> OR <u>OCCURS</u>
<u>IMMEDIATELY</u>:

- Write it on a piece of paper

- Crumple into a ball

- Throw, crush, burn, mutilate, spindle, or otherwise destroy your paper and your "hover trap"

- Say aloud, "I have the controls"

- Followed by, "I have a mission to complete"

- Continue your mission

CHAPTER 14

Finishing Well

Hover Trap #11

Photo 14-1 The mission isn't over until you are on the ground and the rotors stop turning. Until then, calamity can occur in an instant. (Photo by Travis Zielinski)

"Army 428, cleared straight in runway 29, mid-field break, circle to land pad seven. There's no traffic. Call over the numbers."

It was Saturday. Monterey Bay shimmered in front of us. It was always good to be back home. The November sky was clear and the sun was still high in the sky. We had just finished three weeks of combat exercises in the Mojave Desert.

I wasn't a very popular guy right now. The rest of my unit arrived home the day before with instructions to clean and service all the equipment. It was my decision to have them work Saturday even after being gone for most of November and celebrating Thanksgiving in a tent. My crew stayed an extra day for an after action review.

"Fritzsche advisory, 428 is at the numbers."

Looking down during the overhead break, I could see my men looking back. If all went as planned, we would taxi old 428 up to the wash rack, shut down, and let the maintenance folks service her. I wanted to inspect my platoon leader's equipment. We were part of a rapid deployable unit, meaning we could get called anytime to go anywhere.

Recovery and Review is by far the easiest phase of this process to let slip, approach half heartedly, and not execute fully.

Regardless of what we had just done, I wanted to be ready for the next mission. Before I could release the men, I wanted to know the status of a few things:

- The Aircraft: How many were flyable, which ones needed maintenance, what parts were on order and when the broken aircraft would be flyable. All the aircraft washed and secured for the weekend.
- Vehicles: Maintenance completed, serviced, cleaned, and secured in the motor pool.
- All weapons: Accounted for, cleaned, and secured in the armory.
- Night Vision Devices: Accounted for, serviced, cleaned, and secured in the armory.
- Other equipment: Cleaned, serviced, secured in the unit storage area.

I wasn't a very popular guy but that was the life of a rapid deployable air assault unit: training, deployment, execution, and recovery.

Recovery and Review discipline centers on mastering the art of finishing well. Recovery and Review is by far the easiest phase of this process to not execute fully. It is not glamorous; it's the grunt work, and it's hard work at that. If we complete it haphazardly, we have made the decision to settle for less in life. Completed diligently, it will set us up for success time and time again.

The mission isn't completed until recovery is done. If it isn't done well, it will negatively affect the execution on the next iteration of the training, deployment, execution, and recovery cycle.

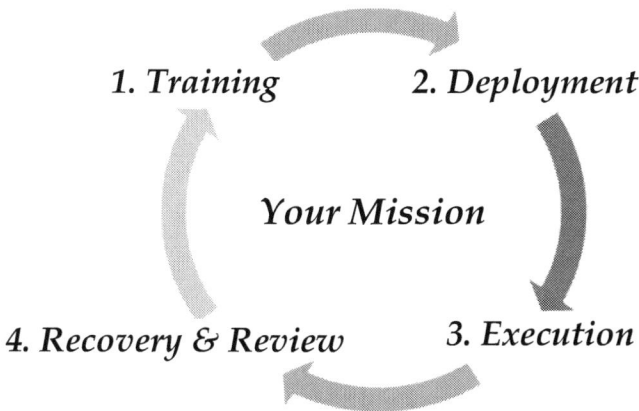

1. Training   2. Deployment

Your Mission

4. Recovery & Review   3. Execution

Figure 14-1 Your Mission Life Cycle diagram

By not finishing well, an individual or organization starts a downward spiral that will take much more effort to correct later than if dealt with immediately.

Do you remember in Part I we learned and applied the concept of effective translational lift? As a quick reminder of this aerodynamic phenomenon, the key points are:

- It's caused by the front of the rotor disk being in clean air while the back portion is in dirty air.
- It occurs at a speed of about 15 – 25 mph.
- It is accompanied by a very noticeable shaking of the airframe.
- If not anticipated, the nose of the aircraft will rise and turn to the right.
- But if anticipated, the helicopter will fly through it and there will be a huge, up to 30%, increase in efficiency of the rotor system.

The same dynamic occurs in reverse when a helicopter is slowing down to land. As the helicopter flares to decelerate, the rear of the rotor disk starts to catch the turbulent air produced by the front but the rotor disk is still in clean air. Again, there is a shaking of the aircraft.

If not anticipated, the biggest consideration during this last phase of flight is the immediate loss of the efficiency ETL provides. If power is not applied while leaving ETL, the aircraft will drop significantly and, depending on the type of helicopter, will cause a hard landing at best or a crash at worst.

Once again at a hover, the aircraft is using brute force to lift its weight as well as swimming upstream, accelerating the air already pouring into the rotor system due to the vortices. Finishing well is energy intensive but sets up future success because so few do it well. You will do it well.

> *Most people and organizations don't finish well. They see the end and think their momentum will take them to the finish line.*

Just like the landing phase, leaving ETL, and completing your mission successfully, finishing well in all aspects of your personal and professional life will also set you up for future successes.

Most people and organizations don't finish well. They see the end and think their momentum will take them to the finish line.

They are tempted to pack it in and worry about recovery later. They feel momentum can take them the rest of the way. However, have you ever seen a champion runner walk over the finish line? I haven't either and it's because they know how important it is to be fully committed to the very end.

From the beginning of this book we've talked about how getting out of the hover trap is a sustainable, repeatable process that battles our very human nature to stay stuck, stationary, and possibly ineffective.

Hover **Check**

✦ Can you remember a time you did not finish well?

✦ How did it affect your next assignment? What were the implications?

✦ Think about a project, assignment, or goal you are working toward. Do you see opportunities where planning to finish well will have a long-term beneficial effect on you, the people around you and how you think about yourself?

✦ If so, take time to plan how you will counteract the natural tendency to let up before your mission is complete.
    1.
    2.
    3.
    4.
    5.

✦ Now, contact your wingman and let them know you are planning to stop only when you are complete.

EMERGENCY PROCEDURE 14

IF YOU SEE YOUR GOAL IN SIGHT AND EXPERIENCE A SUDDEN LOSS OF POWER IMMEDIATELY:

✦ Know you are not finishing well

✦ Gather all your focus

✦ Grind out the task until completed

✦ Remember: Training, Deployment, Execution, Recovery & Review

✦ Know professionals only stop when the mission is complete

PART III

Getting Out of Your Hover Trap

Photo III-1 You're not a leader if nobody follows you. Every takeoff signals the end of an intense period of preparation and planning. (Courtesy US Army)

"The question isn't who is going to let me; it's who is going to stop me."

- Ayn Rand

It's critical that we understand the dynamics of hovering and the hover traps we fall into but just identifying them isn't enough. It's fine to discuss theories and examples, the "what" of being productive and successful.

Now it's time to discuss the "how" of it.

- How do I transform busy into effective?
- How do I get from where I am to where I want to be?
- How do I become more self-directed in every important aspect of my life?
- How do I become more truthful with myself about the causes of the situations I'm in?
- Once I identify what trap I'm in, how do I get out of it?
- How do I avoid falling back into the same, or a different, trap again?

This book would be incomplete without addressing how to lay out a simple, step-by-step, repeatable, and sustainable process for getting you, a loved one, or your organization out of a hover and on with a productive, satisfying, and fulfilled life.

Hopefully by now the concepts and exercises have already allowed you to see things differently, to be truthful enough with yourself to say, "Yes, I do that all the time." An accurate self-perception is very powerful. An inaccurate self-perception is just as powerful but incredibly more devastating. You cannot allow it to exist in your plan to escape from your hover trap.

We are now ready to get into it with these concepts. It won't be easy, fun or without discomfort. But I promise you the price is too high and the benefit too great to not act decisively NOW. I encourage you to do the hard work. By systemizing it, you will be able to apply this planning tool over and over again.

The exercises in this book will deliver this: By following the process laid out in the next chapter, you WILL break through the barriers keeping you in your personal hover trap, helping you to be effective while accomplishing your mission.

CHAPTER 15

Goals First

"Amateurs talk tactics, professionals talk logistics."

- *Military Axiom*

Tactics equal execution. Logistics refers to planning. Planning is the unglamorous, often tedious, part of success. We don't put the time into proper planning because we're focused on the stimulating, fun execution portion. Interestingly, when we apply more effort to prepare for an endeavor, we only ensure the execution is nearly flawless, building momentum and credibility while, at the same time, setting us up for success with more opportunities.

Photo 15-1 Excellent planning leads to excellent mission outcomes. (Courtesy US Army)

When you plan complex night operations, coordinate numerous aviation assets, artillery, and ground forces, you require the same skills and competencies you use accomplishing positive action in all aspects of your life. Goal-setting is the key to success in any endeavor and is worth taking the time to do.

Dr. Gail Matthews, a professor of Psychology at Dominican University in California, was interested in this subject and started doing research. She quickly found references to a famous and often quoted "Yale Goals Study of 1953." It was referenced online and in books 6,220 times when I checked on Google. (I guess you can add one more book reference.)

The premise of the study went like this: Members of the Yale class of 1953 who formulated written goals over time became more successful, earning 10 times more income than those who only thought about their goals or didn't have any. In 1996, *Fast Company* researched the study to find it had never happened. It was an urban legend. This motivated Dr. Matthews to conduct her own Goals Research Study. (Gail Matthews, 2007) The results are powerful. Let me first explain how the research project was designed and then we will talk in more detail about the study's implications for getting more accomplished, faster.

267 participants were recruited from numerous sources including businesses, organizations, and business networking groups. 149 participants completed the study. Of that number, the ages ranged from 23 to 72, with 37 males and 112 females. They were from all over the world and from mixed backgrounds. The countries represented included the United States, Belgium, England, India, Australia, and Japan. The background of the participants included "a variety of entrepreneurs, educators, healthcare professionals, attorneys, artists, bankers, marketers, human services providers, managers, vice presidents, directors of non-profits and others."

Participants were randomly assigned to one of five groups:
- **Group 1** – Unwritten Goals
- **Group 2** – Written Goals
- **Group 3** – Written Goals and Action Plans

- **Group 4** – Written Goals, Action Plans, A Friend or Trusted Advisor
- **Group 5** – Written Goals, Action Plans, Progress Reports to a Friend or Trusted Advisor

Group 1 members were asked to Think about their goals (what they wanted to accomplish over the next four weeks) and then asked to rate that goal on the following dimensions:

- Difficulty
- Importance
- The extent to which they had the Skills and Resources to accomplish the goal
- Their Commitment and Motivation to reach the goal
- Whether or not they had pursued this goal before and, if so, their prior success

Members in **Groups 2 – 5** were asked to write (type into the online survey) their goals and then to rate their goals on the same dimensions above.

Group 3 was also asked to formulate action plans for their goals.

Group 4 was asked to formulate action plans and send their goals and plans to a trusted friend or advisor.

Group 5 was asked to formulate action plans and send their goals, action plans, and weekly progress reports to a trusted friend or advisor. This group was also sent weekly reminders to email quick progress reports to their friend or advisor.

After four weeks, all group members were asked to record their progress and determine the degree to which they had accomplished their goals. The types of goals were not insignificant. A wide variety of goals were represented. Here is a list, in order of most to least mentioned, of the type of goal:

- ✦ Completing a project
- ✦ Increasing income
- ✦ Increasing productivity
- ✦ Getting organized
- ✦ Enhancing performance/achievement
- ✦ Enhancing life balance
- ✦ Reducing work anxiety and learning a new skill

Figure 15-1

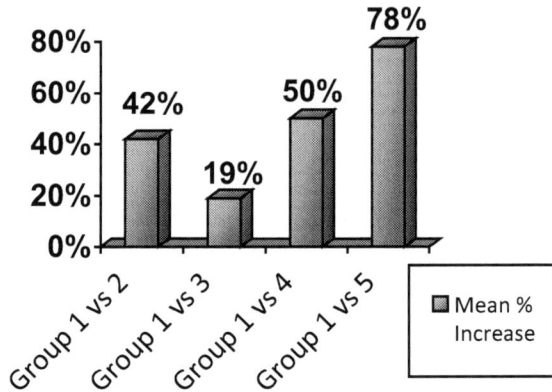

Examples of completing a project included writing a chapter of a book, updating a website, listing and selling a house, completing a strategic plan, securing a contract, hiring employees, and preventing a hostile take-over. By no means are these trivial tasks, like taking out the garbage or mowing the lawn.

Figure 15-1 shows the benefit of writing our goals down as opposed to just thinking about them. In the study, this produced a 42% increase in mean goal achievement. That's a 42% increase from Group 1 compared to Group 2; significant!

Additionally, there was an incredible 78% increase in mean goal achievement when comparing Group 1 to Group 5. Looking at the data another way, using the combined techniques of Group 2 through Group 5, the average goal achievement increased a significant 47%.

Yes, we must live our lives while, at the same time, possess a process for working on them; improving as we go.

This study strongly suggests possessing written goals pays significant dividends. It also provides strong evidence supporting an added benefit when a framework is built around those goals.

We must acknowledge that our lives, like organizations, benefit from both working in and on them. All aspects of our lives can benefit from this construct: We must live our lives while at the same time possess a process for working on them, improving as we go.

Escape the Hover Trap

The Goal Research Study is very important. Not only does it illustrate the importance of goals, it also spells

out a step-by-step plan to accomplish them. I thought it was such a simple process I developed an Apple iPhone mobile application to help you transform busy into effective.

Get it at www.hovertraponline.com. A more detailed explanation of it is in the Hover Trap Resources section of this book.

Hover *Check*

➤ List the goal you want to accomplish and the date it is due.

➤ Goal:

➤ Create an action plan to accomplish the above goal with due dates:
   1.
   2.
   3.
   4.
   5.

➤ Select your wingman:

➤ Set a schedule for regular communication:

CHAPTER 16

Your Mission Plan

Mission, Enemy, Troops Available, Terrain, and **Time Available,** or **METT-T,** is a key planning template for any military commander, regardless of level or size of command. It allows them to quickly get their heads around what is asked of them. It is also the major building block on your journey to transform mere busyness into effectiveness.

It's simple and it works.

It also enables the leader to understand whether they have enough of or the right assets and to find this key piece of information as close to the beginning of the process as possible. It is essential for individuals or organizations to use this process in planning their future actions within their lives and careers.

METT-T has been used successfully for decades in the most stressful, dynamic and chaotic environments on earth: the modern battlefield.

In light of this, I have adapted **METT-T** for your use. You can leverage its time and battle-tested simplicity to create a more powerful and successful life, career or organization. Let's look at this proven model through a new lens.

Mission Enemy Troops Terrain - Time

✣ **Mission**: Instead of planning a military mission, what mission are you planning for your life? Answer these critical questions: Why am I on this earth? How will the world be a better place because I was here? Thoughtful answers to these questions will give you what a lot of people have never known: your purpose. Your mission could and should take years to accomplish. If you can accomplish it too easily, it is not your mission. Decide whether your goal is about your family, friends, health, career, or organization?

o Define the: who, what, where, when, how, and why of your goal.

o Give your goal life and definition so you're not boxing a ghost. Quantify what you want to accomplish. Make it concrete by defining parameters that make it real.

o Write your goals down in a personal and private journal. Share them only with others you trust and ones who will hold you accountable.

o Clearly understand why you want to accomplish this goal. How will it help you in your life?

o What are the specified tasks you'll need to accomplish? This step-by-step action plan, if followed, will lead you to accomplish your mission.

o What does success look like? Again, quantify it. Make it real. What does it look, smell, and feel like? If you can't visualize yourself accomplishing your mission, you have set too ambitious a goal.

Developing your personal mission statement is the first and most important step of the METT-T process. It's your foundation. If you don't invest time in this phase, the rest of your plan will not reflect what you truly want to accomplish. Develop a 100% truthful foundation before you take off on your journey.

Because this is so critical, read through these examples of personal mission statements to give you an idea of what yours might look like:

Career / Business

✦ I want to be the CFO of a privately owned, mid-sized financial services company in Southern California where I can use my experience and expertise to lead the company and to provide for my family. I will accomplish this by December 1, 2011.

Find the who, what, where and why in the above mission statement. Are they all there? The action plan, or the how, follows:

✦ The following actions are required to reach my goal:
   1. Select an accountability partner, mentor or coach to help keep me on track by June 1, 2011.
   2. Identify privately owned mid-sized financial services companies in Southern California by June 15, 2011.
   3. Develop a sketch of the industry sector of the target market to include competitors by July 1, 2011.

4. Research common issues the target companies are facing by July 15, 2011.
5. Produce a one-page professional profile for use during informational interviews by August 1, 2011.
6. Visit or join the appropriate industry associations and get involved to increase visibility and contacts in the target industry by August 20, 2011.
7. Use your personal and professional network to help advertise you to your target industry by August 20, 2011.
8. Schedule informational interviews with target companies by September 1, 2011.
9. Match your skills and past successes to the target companies' needs by September 15, 2011.
10. Develop a report or proposal that highlights your skills, their issues, and how you can solve their problems by October 1, 2011.

Be as detailed as possible when constructing an action plan. Use the free download discussed in the Hover Trap Resources section of this book to help visualize each step. It is easier to make a plan than it is to stick with it. But if you are serious about what you are doing, then it's up to you to do it. If you're waiting to be carried by somebody else, you have already lost the battle.

Health

✦ I will attain my target weight of 175 lbs and improve my general conditioning so I can feel better, have more energy and avoid health complications. I will do this for myself and as a commitment to my wife and children. I will lose 25 lbs by Oct 1, 2011.

Find the, who, what, where and why in the above mission statement. Are they all there? And again, the action plan, or the how, follows:

⚜ The following actions are required to reach my goal:

1. Tell a close friend or get a workout partner to help me execute my plan by April 1, 2011.
2. Get fitted for a proper pair of running shoes by April 5, 2011.
3. Research or create a workout schedule by April 15, 2011.
4. Join a gym or boot camp that fits my schedule by April 15, 2011.
5. Create a chart to record the date and weight by April 15, 2011. Record weight at the same time of the day on the same day once a week.
6. Cut caffeine to one cup a day and reduce alcohol intake by April 20, 2011.
7. Exercise at least five times a week and run three miles at least three times a week by May 1, 2011.

You might notice each action plan has the four critical elements identified in the Goals Research Study in Chapter 15: Goals written down, a written action plan, an accountability partner, mentor, wingman or coach, and regular communication with them.

Now it's your turn. I have provided you with a template for your personal mission statement. Let's create it. You have the controls.

Personal Mission Statement for _____

Remember to answer the who, what, where, why, and when questions.

I will...

The Action Plan:

Remember to be as detailed as possible and have a due date for every step along the way. I suggest starting with selecting an accountability partner, mentor, wingman or coach.

I will accomplish this by:

1.

Due by:

2.

Due by:

3.

Due by:

4.

Due by:

5.

Due by:

Note: In the Hover Trap Resources section of this book there are instructions for downloading a free file so you can update your plan electronically.

With a well defined, complete personal mission statement the hardest part is over. Remember, the most critical part of the mission statement is to select the right mission for you. That doesn't mean it's the most fun, easiest, or the most intuitive. It's often the exact opposite. Selecting the right mission for you, at this time in your life, must be your highest priority. Everything else is built on it.

Give yourself options. Do you need specialized training? Get it. Afraid to speak in public? Work on it. Need help getting off the dime? Enlist a close friend or hire somebody to get you moving. Whatever the obstacles, resolve to remove them.

The next section of the METT-T process is to examine the enemy inside all of us. This enemy may be the reason we get stuck in our hover traps in the first place. Take a long, hard look inward here.

Mission **Enemy** Troops Terrain - Time

✦ **Enemy**: Most of the time we are our own worst enemy. Have you been your worst enemy? This is the time to take an honest look inward. Remember, we build the cages we live in. What are you fearful of? Are your emotions controlling your actions? If so, it makes sense to step into the Truth Room and examine where you are right now compared to where you want to be in the near future.

✦ Focus on you; often the enemy of you.
  o What do you think is holding you back?
  o What are your weaknesses?
  o Examine your recent activity to determine if your actions support your goals. If they do, great. If they don't, ask yourself, "What am I going to do about it?"
  o Have you identified patterns or habits that consistently derail your go forward plans? If so, use the hover traps in part II to help identify them.
  o Determine possible courses of action. Give yourself options. Do you need specialized training? Get it. Afraid to speak in public? Work on it. Need help getting off the dime? Enlist a close friend or hire somebody to get you moving. Whatever the obstacles, resolve to remove them.
  o If you need to go back to your action plan and modify it, do so. It's a working document, a plan for your success. Do what you need to do.

With my clients, I have seen some of the most dramatic realizations in this area. This is where, if you are truthful with yourself, you can reveal answers to lifelong questions. What is so awesome about it? Whether you finally acknowledge a hover behavior or discover one for the first time, it changes the trajectory of your thoughts about yourself, others, and what is possible.

On the following pages are some examples:

Family
  o With my child, I react too swiftly, without all the facts, damaging the relationship and building resentment.

- o I don't leave room for others to have what I consider a valid opinion. They are always wrong and I am right, resulting in a closing-down effect with interaction.
- o I consistently prioritize other things above my family, leaving them feeling they don't matter to me.

Career / Business
- o I would rather die than give a presentation in front of my colleagues, making me pass up opportunities beneficial to my standing in the company.
- o I'm a great starter, but a horrible finisher. I'm afraid it is affecting people's opinion of me.
- o When faced with opposition I freeze, become very cautious, afraid to make a misstep. This hurts my job performance and ability to be promoted.
- o I am not the kind of leader I want to be. I get things done so aggressively that I leave a wake of human destruction in my path. This inability to work well with others and build a healthy team will limit me professionally.

Spiritual
- o After accomplishing so much in my life I feel hollow and empty inside. There must be more to life than just making money.
- o I once had a certain capacity for compassion and forgiveness in me. I don't know what's happened, but I feel I'm becoming cynical and bitter.
- o I don't help people anymore.

You can see why you would not want these examples announced to the public. However, you need to address them.

That is why it's so important to pick the right mentor, advisor or coach. It's also critical to structure your action plan in such a way as to counteract these behaviors.

The Enemy Within

What is holding you back?
- o   **Family Life:**

- o   **Friends:**

- o   **Career / Business:**

- o   **Health:**

- o   **Spiritual Life:**

What are your weaknesses? What do you need to improve?
1.
2.
3.
4.

Note: It's critical your action plan Incorporate activities to improve in these areas. The hardest part is acknowledging them. Congratulations!

Using the hover traps as a guide while assessing your past with a critical eye is very powerful. This exercise is not about self-loathing or tearing oneself down. It's about embracing reality and uncovering what is tripping you up again and again. It's about being your best you. Only by facing the truth will there ever be any real hope of breaking a cycle that may be keeping you from the peace of mind, success, and accomplishment you desire.

Mission Enemy **Troops** Terrain - Time

- **Troops Available**: Your troops are the assets, skills, and competencies you bring as an individual. It's very common for us to downplay our strengths. We've been taught, "Nobody likes a braggart," so I encourage you to ask close, trusted friends what they think your strengths are. Look at old performance reviews. Think about the things that give you the most personal pleasure and satisfaction. Those are also the things we usually do well. Think about what you believe in. Your principles and beliefs are assets, too.
  - o Write down your hard skills strengths and experiences.
  - o What soft skills do you bring that are uniquely you, which differentiate you from others?
  - o How's your morale? Are you ready to take on this task? Are you mentally up for it?
  - o When you've completed this exercise you should have compiled an impressive list of your hard and soft skills, resources available, and assessed your mental attitude to push forward.

Maybe you've noticed this too. A lot of my clients find it easier to list their perceived weaknesses than their strengths. That's a shame. Unfortunately most of us get stuck on our weaknesses so a lot of our energy goes there. But what about our gifted talents, the things we do extremely well without a lot of effort? Shouldn't we expand those areas, too?

The answer is yes and that's what we'll capture now. Just like I asked you to focus a critical eye on weaknesses in the enemy section, now I want you to focus an equally critical eye on your strengths. It's only fair. Here's what some have said in the past.

Friends
- o   I'm a friend others can count on. I am dependable.
- o   I listen well and offer solid advice when asked.
- o   I'm truthful with my friends.
- o   Usually I'm in an up mood and think people like to be around me.

Career / Business
Hard skills:
- o   Developing and executing strategies.
- o   Analysis of complex problems and courses of action through the use of financial models.
- o   Experience with SAP, Oracle and other enterprise management systems.
- o   Computer literate.

Soft skills:
- o   Excellent team builder.
- o   Manage people well.
- o   Motivate others.
- o   Excellent listening skills.
- o   Experienced at communicating and creating a shared vision for my team.
- o   Can read between the lines regarding team's mood.

o   Morale is high and I have the energy to make change happen.

These are just examples. Ask co-workers or friends as a reality check. Also, look at old performance reviews to get some perspective. Usually, you have strengths that go back to childhood. Don't forget to add them.

Troops Available: Asset Inventory

Strengths in Hard Skills and Experiences:
   1.
   2.
   3.
   4.
   5.

Strengths in Soft Skills:
   1.
   2.
   3.
   4.
   5.

How is your morale? Are you up for this challenge?

Note: Don't limit yourself to five. Add as many as you need.

The Troops Available section should pump you up. I am convinced everybody has valuable and unique skills they bring to the table. It's important to seriously assess your skills and compare them to the skills needed to accomplish your mission. If you find a gap between them, that's GOOD! It will also show you the skills you will need to develop to make your mission a success.

Imagine the waste if you refuse to take the time to determine whether your current skill set matches what you need to accomplish your mission. Talk about a hover trap! You can avoid wasted time, energy, and grief by figuring it out as early in the process as possible.

Mission Enemy Troops **Terrain** - Time

✦ **Terrain**: Instead of hills, valleys, and lakes, think about your external environment, things outside of your control. Miller and Heiman in their book *Large Account Management Process* (Robert Miller, 2005) call it the field of play. For career issues, think about your industry or market position. If you are concentrating on your family or friends, think about how others may relate to you. Where do you fit? How are you perceived as a husband, wife, son, or daughter?

   o   Evaluate where you fit within your industry, company, demographic etc.
   o   Determine if your skills fit within other alternative areas.
   o   Interpersonally, examine how others relate to you. Are there patterns developing? Are they good or bad? Family history is a great place to start. We tend to repeat behaviors learned, often subconsciously, from our childhood.
   o   Examine economic and personal obstacles that you must overcome.

o Search for an avenue of approach that will get you to your goal. What is the path most likely to lead to success?

o As always, write down what you find.

Are you seeing how the METT-T model breaks out essential elements of your situation so we can better examine them? Knowing your field of play or terrain is essential for a successful mission. It's another way of asking, "What's my environment?" I have gathered different examples from different life aspects to spark some thought.

Career/Business

o My industry is in transition. Manufacturing has moved overseas and now a lot of engineering has also moved. Although the US remains an important market, growth is coming from Asia and Latin America.

o Industry consolidation has raised the stakes for players still in the market and has limited the opportunities for advancement.

o Others would consider me a senior manager within my industry. My background supports this.

o I have an MBA, but many people in positions at my level do too. It's not a differentiator anymore. I may be perceived as letting my skills get dated.

o My experience in manufacturing and logistics can be applied in many industries. Alternative energy may be an interesting growth segment to research.

o What would it take to make an industry transition? I have enough saved to devote a year to this shift. (Or, I will have to keep working at my current position while I execute this transition.)

Do the work up front to put the odds in your favor.

As you can see, I have only scratched the surface of the considerations needed to entertain an industry change. Once you start, you will no doubt find many more. Don't be afraid to seek out advice from people who have accomplished what you want to accomplish. A SWOT diagram can be helpful here.

However, this section is not just about careers. It is applicable to all the life aspects you are now familiar with: Family, Friends, Career/Business, Health and Spiritual. Okay, you have the controls:

Terrain: Your Field of Play

Where do you fit within your industry, company, demographic etc?

How else can your skills be employed?

How have you maneuvered in your current space?

Have you ruffled feathers in the past?

What economic or personal obstacles must you overcome?

Do you see any patterns developing, good or bad?

How will you manage the key aspects of your environment while planning to accomplish your mission? Are there certain risks that need to be mitigated?

Taking your field of play into consideration, do you see a unique avenue of approach getting to where you want to be?

Note: Taking the time to consider your external environment will allow you to develop contingencies when things don't go as planned.

Knowing your terrain or field of play and where you are within it can mean the difference between a successful mission and a mission abort. Do the work up front to put the odds in your favor.

Mission Enemy Troops Terrain - **Time**

 ✦ **Time Available**: Everything needs to be bound by a time limit. Goals must possess a definite time limit or difficult and unwanted tasks will be put off indefinitely. Remember, it's human nature to seek and stay static in our comfort zone, hover, equilibrium, etc. There are precious few things that can never be replaced and time is one of them.
   - Time or the lack of it is often the impetus for action.
   - Carve out time to prepare your plan — a little every day.
   - As a rule of thumb, use the 1/3 - 2/3 rule: Use 1/3 of the time you have to plan and the remaining 2/3 for the execution of your plan.
   - Make a schedule and stick to it!

Acknowledging the time element is such an important part of the process. Without it we can easily get stuck in the Analyzed and Paralyzed trap. In our minds, it's important and will get done someday.

Someday is not good enough! It needs to be now. Creating a schedule of events not only creates structure around this complex project, it also creates a sense of urgency to get it completed. I have added tools in the Hover Resources section in the back of the book to assist you in making a plan and sticking to it.

A lot of people say, "Life is too short" when struggling with challenges. I don't agree. If you have found yourself in an unhealthy relationship, among dubious friends, stuck in a horrible work situation, suffering from serious health issues, or lacking a relationship with your God, life isn't too short, it's too long. Nothing makes time slow more than facing adversity without a plan, and alone.

Don't be *that* person.

Using METT-T, know:

o   Your personal mission
o   The enemy within
o   Your troops available or assets
o   Your terrain or environment
o   The time available for both planning and execution

You will have exponentially increased your odds of success while giving yourself a repeatable system. It's the system that will give you a competitive advantage in whatever aspect of your life you choose.

Now, *that's* the person you want to be.

CHAPTER 17

Into the Clean Air

Many times in my flying and business career I have prepared and planned. I have thought of every contingency and even the contingency to the contingency. I checked, double checked and

> *"...and, as always, keep the faith."*
> - *Tavis Smiley*

rechecked the double check, all to find the hard work had been done. Every aspect of the preparation had been completed and there was only one thing left to do: execute the mission.

You should feel that way now.

Right now, your mission is the most important thing. Your mission is to accomplish your life's purpose. Execute it with wild abandon. Be audacious, vibrant and bold. Be confident you have done the hard work, applied the appropriate resources and are armed with the right knowledge.

You have now identified and understand the hover traps that once derailed you. Your awareness of them is heightened. You now anticipate them. You now see the connections between the activities that keep you busy and ineffective. You now have a plan to transform your once wasted energy into effective action to move you forward.

Use the emergency procedures and tools provided here to keep you on course and on glide slope while you launch into your future.

Visit the Truth Room often. The experience will give you clarity and understanding as to why you might be in a hover, why you might want to stay there, and why it's imperative you break out of it into the clean air.

The effects of effective translational lift (ETL) are real but they're inconsequential when anticipated. The boost in efficiency after ETL *is* real and will allow you to have extra power when life happens and you need to sprint. Keep your pace sustainable.

You don't have to do this alone. Every professional who is required to be at their very best has some kind of help. You should too if you want optimum results. Select a mentor, friend, or coach as your wingman. Don't be proud. Trust them. You will soon rely on each other, doing your own version of the Thach Weave, protecting and giving each other support.

Don't be safe. Remember the difference between an adventure and a quest. By committing to getting out of the hover trap, you will risk much but gain even more. You will set yourself on a journey, fundamentally changing you. You may never return to your starting point and you will never be the same. In doing so, you will have avoided the mistakes we're all programmed to make and transformed busy into effective. You will be at once the same but different. You will be stronger.

Now it's launch time. You're the Pilot in Command. You have the controls. Go and accomplish your mission. It's waiting for you in the clean air.

About the Author

Ken Gryske, Director of Business Development at Marcum LLP, helps grow earnings and increase opportunities through an integrated approach to business, organizational and professional development. Marcum LLP is a 150 partner, international accounting and consulting firm headquartered in Melville, New York.

Ken Gryske

Prior to joining the private sector, he received a Regular Army Commission. As an Army Aviator, he commanded a rapid deployable air assault unit.

He earned his MBA from Pepperdine University, is a board certified executive coach and has held positions with national responsibility in sales and business development. Ken delivers entertaining, high-impact lessons from his military and business experience.

He regularly speaks on topics relating to strategy, employee engagement, and business development in Southern California, where he lives with his wife and son.

Phone: 949-257-7325
Email: ken.gryske@marcumllp.com
Web: www.marcumllp.com
LinkedIN: www.linkedin.com/in/kengryske

Escape the Hover Trap

The Hover Trap mobile application was developed to replicate the four key steps of the Goal Research Study conducted by Gail Mathews of Dominican University.

The main landing page is laid out to get you started immediately. It has four buttons: Goal, Action Plan, Wingman, and About.

Pressing the Goal button opens a screen with three main elements. There is a place for your large goal to be written down. A calendar function is provided to give you a due date. The Done button is selected once you have accomplished your goal.

To facilitate communication with your wingman, when the Done button is selected, the application will open a new email to your wingman.

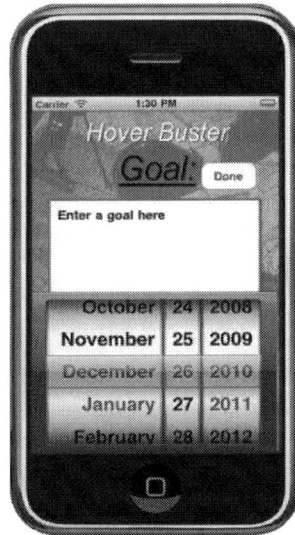

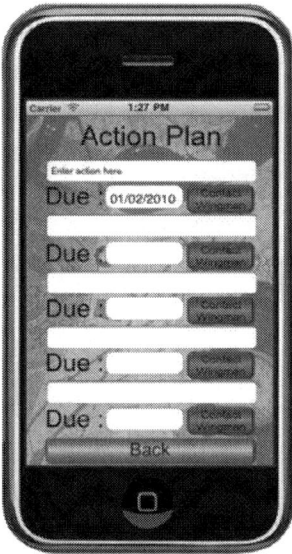

Every goal must have an action plan to support it. By pressing the Action Plan button, you will open a page with spaces to enter five actions that support your main goal. Each has a space for a due date and a Contact Wingman button.

When you push the Contact Wingman button, the application will automatically launch your email program with your wingman's email address already loaded and Hover Trap Goal in the subject line.

The Wingman button facilitates a critical part of the Goals Research Study; communication with a trusted friend, mentor, or coach. Two fields are provided for you to enter the name of your wingman and the email address of your wingman. Pick your wingman carefully.

As mentioned before, whenever you select Done on the goal page or Contact Wingman in your action plan, your email program will automatically open with a new email addressed to your wingman. Just write your progress or note down and select Send.

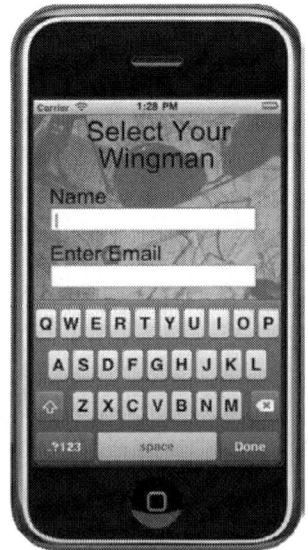

Pillars of Strengths Exercise©

My executive clients constantly amaze me with the highly developed skills and capabilities they possess. It created a challenge in my private practice because many have talents and skills applicable to many different opportunities. In short, some face the enviable dilemma of having too many options or opportunities, forcing them into a hover while they try to figure out which path is the best to take.

Enviable yes, but it's still a problem. To meet this challenge, I developed the **Pillars of Strengths Exercise©**. This exercise is most effective when you need to evaluate multiple opportunities with clarity to determine what is most important. It assists in orienting you toward which goal will work best for you.

Output of Pillars of Strengths show this person values
Organization Cultural Fit over other factors they selected

Think of it as a navigational aid for any project or initiative. In aviation terms, we don't want to take off for New York and end up in El Paso. I don't want you to leave your hover only to end up at an unintended destination. It's frustrating, wastes time and energy, and is counterproductive.

The Pillars of Strengths Exercise© is free to anybody. By logging onto www.hovertraponline.com, you will gain access to an online version of this tool and start a process that will give you clarity regarding your preferred direction.

It's based on what you have decided is important and is completely flexible. By changing the parameters and weighting, you will see how the outcome changes. Complete the exercise as many times as you need. This is a resource for you and your success.

Staying on Schedule

A large part of taking control of any aspect in your life is to create a plan to address it. This powerful yet simple action is often overlooked. In today's world, which is very complicated, it's hard to comprehend how a solution can be so straight forward yet simple.

I believe in it so much I dedicated an entire chapter to the *Goals Study* to prove with research the power of associated thinking that accompanies setting goals. Think about it this way: All planning and goal setting is a project. It's an important project with a possible huge upside for those who have the courage to face their shortcomings or tackle their largest purpose. Let's do more than simply hope for something better. Let's take action.

Even seemingly simple journeys can get complicated. That's why I use a Gantt chart with every one of my private clients. A simple Gantt chart ensures no important task gets missed and left undone. It is also helpful to those people who prefer to process information visually. The Gantt chart does this and is easily modified.

#	Task name	Start date	Duration	Oct 24	Oct 31	Nov 7	Nov 14	Nov 21	Nov 28
1	Vision Phase	10/28/2010	24						
2	Resume Review	10/28/2010	1						
3	Power Stories	10/28/2010	7						
4	Elevator Pitch	11/5/2010	7						
5	References	11/15/2010	7						
6	Associations	11/22/2010	7						
7									

A simple Gantt chart will help keep you on course guaranteeing you don't forget critical elements of your plan

A Gantt chart outlines the tasks of your action plan in a prioritized order with a definitive start and end date. It's a flexible visual tool that "pulls" you along the path of the plan instead of letting you get knocked off course when you don't have one. Like any plan however, you have to do the work. You have to put in the time to deserve the outcome you want.

Like the Pillars of Strengths exercise, you can log onto www.hovertraponline.com and get access to this and other productivity tools.

Hover Trap Terms

Air Assault - The movement of ground-based military forces by helicopters to seize and hold key terrain and to directly engage enemy forces.

Airspeed Indicator - An instrument used in an aircraft to display the craft's airspeed, typically in knots, to the pilot.

Altitude Indicator - An instrument used in an aircraft to display the height above sea level. It is based on the change in barometric pressure at different heights.

Army Aviation – One of 17 official branches of the US Army. The mission of Army Aviation is to find, fix, and destroy the enemy through fire and maneuver and to provide combat, combat service, and combat service support in coordinated operations as an integral member of the combined arms team.

Artificial Horizon - Also known as gyro horizon, or attitude indicator, is an instrument used in an aircraft to inform the pilot of the orientation of the aircraft relative to earth. It indicates pitch (fore and aft tilt) and bank or roll (side to side tilt) and is a primary instrument for flight in instrument meteorological conditions.

Beam Defense Position – Also known as the "Thach Weave", is an aerial combat tactic developed by naval aviator John S. Thach at the beginning of WWII. It emphasizes teamwork over aircraft agility. It is still an effective tactic today.

Best Rate of Climb Airspeed – Is where the most aerodynamic airspeed of the aircraft is coupled with the maximum power available, resulting in the greatest change in attitude per unit of time. See Maximum Endurance Airspeed.

Brown Out – A term used to describe the effects of blowing dust or sand by the rotor wash of a helicopter, causing the pilots to lose sight of the ground. It is most dangerous during take-off and landing modes of flight when the aircraft is close to the ground.

Career Path - Progress through a career: a planned progression of jobs within an organization or in a professional field leading to the realization of career goals.

Cockpit Scan - The act an aviator takes to systematically look at the flight instruments to maintain a mental picture of where the aircraft is within space and time. Effective for maintaining situational awareness, especially while flying in the clouds or at night.

DABDA - Denial, Anger, Bargaining, Depression, and Acceptance, also known as the stages of grief or loss.

Deck Landing Qualification – The act of learning and demonstrating proficiency in the terminology, procedures and actions of operating an aircraft from and around US Navy ships.

Effective Translational Lift (ETL) – An aerodynamic phenomenon unique to helicopter flight, occurring when leaving or entering hovering flight. While leaving hovering flight at approximately 15 – 27 mph the rotor system is in both smooth and turbulent air causing significant vibration, a roll to the right, and the nose to pitch up.

Emergency Procedure - A series of immediate actions required to maintain control of the aircraft long enough to isolate the malfunction and effect a safe landing. Annotated in the check list with black and white stripes, most are required to be memorized.

Equilibrium - Equilibrium is the condition of a system in which competing influences are balanced.

FM Homing - A selectable function activating a needle in the cockpit to point to the source of a frequency modulated (FM) transmission. Used when radio contact is established but physical location is not.

Fort Rucker, Alabama – Home of Army Aviation and the location of the US Army Flight School.

Gantt Chart - A type of bar chart that illustrates a project schedule. Gantt charts illustrate the start and finish dates of the terminal elements and summary elements of a project.

Global Positioning System - A space-based global navigation satellite system (GNSS) that provides extremely accurate location and time information in all weather and at all times and anywhere on or near the Earth when and where there is an unobstructed line of sight to four or more GPS satellites. It is maintained by the United States government and is freely accessible by anyone with a GPS receiver. Prior to GPS, tactical navigation was accomplished with 1:50,000 maps and WWII Doppler technology.

High Multitasker - One who is engaged in five or more activities at one time in an attempt to be more productive.

Hippocampus - A major component of the brains of humans and other mammals. It belongs to the limbic system and plays important roles in the consolidation of information from short-term memory to long-term memory and spatial navigation. It is known as the "filing cabinet" of the brain.

Horizontal Situation Indicator - An aircraft instrument normally mounted below the artificial horizon in place of a conventional heading indicator. It combines a heading indicator with a VOR/ILS display, reducing pilot workload by lessening the number of elements in the pilot's instrument scan to the six basic flight instruments.

Hover - The process by which an object is suspended by a physical force against gravity in a stable position without solid physical contact. A helicopter hovering is an extremely inefficient but often useful mode of flight.

Hover Check – Conducted to compare planned and actual aircraft performance. All systems are monitored for proper operation prior to launching on the actual mission. Final check to ensure the aircraft is capable of accomplishing the assigned mission.

Hover Trap – Term used to describe a person's or organization's actions, habits, or beliefs that block positive progress. A bad habit derailing one from their intended goal.

Hover Trap Mobile Application – An application developed to model the findings of the Goal Research Study conducted by Gail Mathews for Dominican University. Entitled, *Hover Trap*, it can be downloaded at www.hovertraponline.com.

"I have the controls" – Essential part of effective cockpit crew coordination known as a three-way positive transfer of control of an aircraft. (Yes, aircraft have crashed because each pilot thought the other was flying.)

Knots Indicated Airspeed (KIAS) – Unit of speed used in aeronautics and based on the nautical mile instead of statute miles per hour used in US cars. One nautical mile equals: 1.15078 statute mile.

Landing Zone (LZ) – Designated helicopter landing area used during Air Assault operations. Selected for a number of reasons, multiple landing zones may be utilized depending on the immediate tactical situation.

Long Range Surveillance Detachment (LRSD) – A detachment of highly trained soldiers, organic to the military intelligence battalion at division level, who perform Long Range Surveillance. The leaders are airborne and Ranger-qualified. All other personnel in the detachment are airborne qualified. Replaced in 2009 by Long Range Surveillance Companies.

Low Multitasker – One engaged in one or two activities at a time to increase productivity.

Maximum Endurance Airspeed – The airspeed where fuel consumption is the least. This occurs at the most aerodynamic airspeed of the aircraft with enough power applied to maintain level flight. NOTE: Maximum Endurance Airspeed and Best Rate of Climb airspeed occur at the same speed. One uses the maximum power available to climb and the other uses the minimum power to maintain flight. See Best Rate of Climb Airspeed.

METT-T – Mission, Enemy, Terrain, Troops and Time Available. Used as a framework for mission analysis and planning. We have adapted this battle-proven process for use in personal development.

Nap of the Earth (NOE) - Is a type of very low-altitude flight course used by military aircraft to avoid enemy detection and attack in a high-threat environment. During NOE flight, geographical features are used as cover, exploiting valleys and folds in the terrain by flying in, rather than over, them. This keeps the aircraft below enemy radar coverage, avoiding being silhouetted. Other terms are also used, including "ground-hugging," "terrain masking," or "flying under the radar."

Natural Selection – How nature weeds out the weak. It is the process by which biological traits become more or less common in a population due to consistent effects upon the survival or reproduction of their bearers. It is a key mechanism of evolution.

Night Vision Goggles (NVG) - Is an optical instrument that allows images to be produced in levels of light approaching total darkness. They intensify existing light by 2500% or more. They are most often used by the military and law enforcement agencies but are available to civilian users. The term usually refers to a complete unit, including an image intensifier tube, a protective and generally water-resistant housing, and some type of mounting system.

Personal Development - Refers to activities that improve self-knowledge and identity, develop talents and potential, build human capital and employability, enhance quality of life, and contribute to the realization of dreams and aspirations.

Pillars of Strength – A software-aided exercise developed by Spero Strategies LLC, to help people determine what is important to them and how it is prioritized on a weighted decision matrix. A version for a free download can be found at www.hovertraponline.com.

Pilot in Command – Is a skill, not rank designation, and is the person aboard the aircraft who is ultimately responsible for its operation and safety during flight. The PIC is the person legally in charge of the aircraft and its flight safety and operation and would normally be the primary person liable for an infraction of any flight rule.

Punctuated Equilibrium - In 1972, paleontologists Niles Eldredge and Stephen Jay Gould published a landmark paper developing this theory and called it Punctuated Equilibria. Opposed to Phyletic Gradualism, which proposes species are in a continuous, steady, "stately unfolding" of nature, Punctuated Equilibrium proposes species spend most of their time in a state of equilibrium, which only rarely and after some external force is set into a rapid growth stage full of adaptation. The author proposes humans, in regard to personal development, react in much the same way.

Punctuated Focus – A term used to describe how to be more productive by intensely focusing on the task at hand and only breaking focus for short mental breaks. Akin to an athlete flexing his muscles during a workout and resting between exercises.

Rapid Deployable Unit – A military unit capable of quickly deploying its forces. They are normally assigned geographic areas of coverage and specific mission scenarios. Such forces typically consist of elite military units and may receive priority in equipment and training to prepare them for their mission.

Rappel Master – Person responsible for rigging an aircraft for rappel operations. Ensures ropes are deployed and personnel are attached correctly. They are in charge of deploying personnel from the aircraft and use hand signals to communicate with the personnel who will be rappelling. It is a requirement they carry a sharp knife or axe to cut away a snagged rope or person if the situation endangers the aircraft.

Reserve Officer Training Corp (ROTC) - Is a college-based, officer commissioning program, predominantly in the United States. It is designed as a college elective that focuses on leadership development, problem solving, strategic planning, and professional ethics.

Rotor System - Is a type of fan that is used to generate both the aerodynamic lift force that supports the weight of the helicopter and the thrust that counteracts aerodynamic drag in forward flight. Each main rotor is mounted on a vertical mast over the top of the helicopter as opposed to a helicopter tail rotor, which is connected through a combination of drive shaft(s) and gearboxes along the tail boom. A helicopter's rotor is generally made up of two or more rotor blades. The blade pitch is typically controlled by a swash plate connected to the helicopter flight controls.

Settling with Power – Also known as Vortex Ring State, it is a hazardous condition encountered in helicopter flight. It occurs when the helicopter has three things occurring: A high rate of descent, airspeed lower than effective translational lift, and the helicopter using a large portion of its available power. Applying more power increases the rate of descent.

Spatial Disorientation - Is a condition in which an aircraft pilot's perception of direction does not agree with reality. While it can be brought on by disturbances or disease within the vestibular system, it is more typically a temporary condition resulting from flight into poor weather conditions with low or no visibility. Under these conditions the pilot may be deprived of an external visual horizon, which is critical to maintaining a correct sense of up and down while flying.

Striatum – Part of the brain. In humans the striatum is activated in the presence of stimuli associated with reward but also in the presence of aversive, novel, unexpected, or intense stimuli and cues associated with such events.

Target Fixation – A type of spatial disorientation, it is a process by which the brain is focused so intently on an observed object that awareness of other obstacles or hazards can diminish. Also, in an avoidance scenario, the observer can become so fixated on the target that she will forget to take the necessary action to avoid it, thus colliding with the object.

Thach Weave - Also known as the "Beam Defense Position," it is an aerial combat tactic developed by naval aviator John S. Thach at the beginning of WWII. It emphasizes teamwork over aircraft agility. It is still an effective tactic today. See Beam Defense Position.

Truth Room – Developed by Amy Julian, an organizational development professional, the "Truth Room" is a place in one's mind where one must be honest and frank with oneself. It is used to honestly dialogue through important issues in one's life.

UH-60 Blackhawk - Is a four-bladed, twin-engine, medium-lift utility helicopter manufactured by Sikorsky Aircraft. The UH-60A entered service with the Army in 1979 to replace the Vietnam era Bell UH-1 Iroquois as the Army's tactical transport helicopter. Many upgrades have been implemented since then with the UH-60 now providing the backbone of the Army's medium lift capability.

Unitasking – The act of very deeply focusing on one task at a time to ensure comprehension and increase the ability to recall detailed information quickly.

Vertical Speed Indicator (VSI) - Is one of the flight instruments in an aircraft used to inform the pilot of the near instantaneous (rather than averaged) rate of descent or climb, usually calibrated in feet per minute. In powered flight, the pilot makes frequent use of the VSI to ascertain level flight is being maintained, especially during turning maneuvers.

Vortex / Vortices - Is a spinning, often turbulent, flow of fluid (for our purposes, air). Any spiral motion with closed streamlines is vortex flow. The motion of the fluid swirling rapidly around a center is called a vortex. The speed and rate of rotation of the fluid in a free vortex are greatest at the center, and decrease progressively with distance from the center whereas the speed of a forced (rotational) vortex is zero at the center and increases proportional to the distance from the center.

Vortex Ring State – See Settling with Power.

Wingman - Is a pilot who supports another in a potentially dangerous flying environment. Wingman was originally a term referring to the plane flying beside and slightly behind the lead plane in an aircraft formation. The idea behind the wingman is to add the element of mutual support to aerial combat. A wingman makes the flight both offensive and defensive by increasing fire power, situational awareness, and attacking an enemy threatening a comrade. At least one wingman is required to employ the Thach Weave tactic.

WTF Moment – Identifies a moment one reaches during a time of frustration, stress, and burnout from many attempts to unlock the door with no results. Coined by Mike Brenhaug, it is the title of his book, *WTF – Transform What Appears Negative into a Positive to Become Unstoppable.*

Works Cited

Allen Kevin www.armyaircrews.com/cobra_nam.html [Online] // Army Aircrews. - Dec 31, 2010. - http://www.armyaircrews.com.

Blair Gary Ryan *Self-Reliance* = *Freedom* [Online]. - September 7, 2010. - October 10, 2010.

Brenhaug *WTF: Transform What Appears Negative into a Positive to Become Unstoppable* [Book]. - Foothill Ranch : [s.n.], 2011.

Clifford Nass Eyal Ophir, Anthony Wanger "Cognitive control in media multitaskers" [Journal] // *Proceedings of the National Academy of Sciences*. - 2009. - p. August 24.

Coffman L., Valentine, M. *Slay the E-mail Monster* [Book]. - Charleston, SC : Contact: 951-677-8203, 2010.

Covey S. *First Things First* [Book]. - NY : Fireside, 1995.

DeLong Thomas / Sara "The Paradox of Excellence" [Article] // *Harvard Business Review*. - June 2011. - pp. 119-123.

Dougherty Michael J. "Why Are We Getting Taller As A Species?" [Article] // *Scientific American*. - June 29, 1998.

Ferriss Tim *The 4-Hour Workweek: Escape 9-5, live anywhere, and join the new rich* [Book]. - NY : Crown Publishers, 2007.

FM 1-301 Aeromedical Training for Flight Personnel, Dept of Army Chapter 9: Spatial Disorientation // FM 1-301 *Aeromedical Training for Flight Personnel*. - Washington : Dept of the Army, May 29, 1987.

FM 1-203 Fundamentals of Flight, Dept of Army, HQ FM1-203 *Fundamentals of Flight*. - Washington : Department of the Army, September 9, 1983.

Friedman James "The Myth of the Statges of Dying, Death and Grief" [Journal] // *Skeptic*. - 2008. - p. Volume 14.

Gail Matthews PhD *Goals Research Study* [Report]. - [s.l.] : Dominican University - California, 2007.

Gibbons JJ Katzenbach NB *Confronting Confinement* [Report]. - [s.l.] : The Commission on Safety and Abuse in America's Prisons, 2006.

Glines Carroll *The Doolittle Raiders* [Book]. - NY : Crown Publishers, 1989.

Johnson Spencer *Who Moved My Cheese?* [Book]. - New York : G.P. Putnam's Sons, 2002.

Konrath Sara "Changes in Dispositional Empathy Over Time in American College Students: A meta-Analysis" [Report]. - [s.l.] : University of Michigan, 2010.

Kubler-Ross Elisabeth *On Death and Dying* [Book]. - New York : Simon & Schuster, 1969.

Kumashiro Madoka, Rusbult Caryl E. and Finkcl Eli J. "Navigating Personal and Relational Concerns: The Quest for Equilibrium" [Article] // *Journal of Personality and Social Psychology*. - Vol. 95 No. 1, 2008. - pp. 94-110.

Lally P., van Jaarsveld C.H.M., Potts H., and Wardle, J. "How are habits formed: Modeling habit formation in the real world" [Journal] // *European Journal of Social Pyschology*. - 2009. - pp. 998-1009.

Langley Ann "Between "Paralysis by Analysis" and "Extinction by Instinct" [Journal] // *Sloan Management Review.* - 1995. - pp. 63 - 76.

Matthews Chris *Hardball* [Book]. - NY : Touchstone, 1999.

Marois R., Ivanoff J. "Isolation of a Control Bottleneck of Information Processing with Time-Resolved fMRI" [Journal] // *Trends in Cognitive Sciences.* - 2005. - pp. 296-305.

McLellan A.T., Lewis D.C., O'Brien C.P., Kleber H.D. "Drug dependence, a chronic medical illness: Implications for treatment, insurance, and outcomes evaluation" [Journal] // *JAMA.* - 2000. - pp. 1689-1695.

Melchor Antunano M.D. FAA Pilots Training [Online] // www.faa.gov. - June 1, 2010. - September 26, 2010. - www.faa.gov/pilots/training/airman_eductiona/aerospace_physiology/index.cfm.

National Museum of the United States Air Force *U.S. Air Force Fact Sheet: Doolittle Raid* [Online] // National Museum of the United States Air Force. - December 11th, 2010. - http://www.nationalmuseum.af.mil/.

Poldrack R.A., Foerde L., Knowlton B.J. "Distraction modulates the engagement of competing memory systems." [Journal] // *Proceeding of the National Academy of Sciences.* - 2006. - pp. 11779-83.

Miller Robert, Heiman Stephan, Tuleja Tad *The New Successful Large Account Management: Maintaining and Growing your Most Important Assets - Your Customers* [Book]. - New York : Time Warner Business Books, 2005.

Rosen Christine "The Myth of Multitasking" [Journal] // *The New Atlantis.* - 2008. - pp. 105-110.

Rosenblatt Roger "The Rugged Individual Rides Again" [Article] // *Time*. - October 15, 1984. - p. 1984.

Gould S.J. and Eldredge Niles "Punctuated Equilibria: An Alternative to Phyletic Gradualism" [Article] // *Models In Paleobiology*. - 1972. - pp. 82-115.

Saint-Exupery Antoine de *The Little Prince* [Book]. - New York : Reynal & Hitchcock, Harcourt Brace Jovanonich, Inc., 1943.

Setty Rajesh *Rajesh Setty: Bringing Ideas to Life. With Love!* [Online] // Rajesh Setty Official Website. - 3 14, 2010. - 10 3, 2010. - http://www.rajeshsetty.com/2010/03/14/why-some-smart-people-dont-take-action/.

Smithstein Samantha "Are today's youth even more self-absorbed (and less caring) than generations before?" [Online] // Phychologytoday.com. - June 5, 2010. - September 2, 2010. - http://www.psychologytoday.com/blog/what-the-wild-things-are/201006/are-today-s-youth-even-more-self-absorbed-and-less-caring-gener.

Tracy Brian *Success Leaves Tracks* [Online] // www.briantracy.com. - December 23, 2008. - Jan 5, 2011. - www.briantracy.com/blog/personal-success/success-leaves-tracks.

UH-60A Operators Manual, Dept of Army, HQ TM 1-1520-237-10 [Article] // *Operators Manual for UH-60A, UH-60L, and EH-60A*. - October 31, 1996 updated 2002. - pp. 7-19.

Whitman I.B. and Cohen A. Isaac *Newton, The Principia, A new translation* [Book]. - Berkeley : University of California press, 1999.

Vaknin Sam *Malignant Self Love: Marcissism Revisted* [Book]. - Skopje, Republic of Macedonia : Lidija Rangelovska, 2007.